The Way of Melchizedek

Thomas L. Cossette

Copyright © 2003 by Thomas L. Cossette

The Way of Melchizedek
by Thomas L. Cossette

Printed in the United States of America

ISBN 1-591606-82-9

All rights reserved. No part of this publication may be reproduced or transmitted in any form or by any means without written permission of the publisher.

Unless otherwise indicated, Bible quotations are taken from The King James Version.

Xulon Press
www.XulonPress.com

Xulon Press books are available in bookstores everywhere, and on the Web at www.XulonPress.com.

Table of Contents

Introduction vii

PART I

Chapter 1	Jacob's Understanding 11
Chapter 2	The Coming Promise 27
Chapter 3	The Stars of Heaven 33
Chapter 4	The King of Kings 51
Chapter 5	The Southern Cross 69
Chapter 6	The Gulf of the Serpent 77
Chapter 7	The Way 89
Chapter 8	The Dragon's Flood 97
Chapter 9	The Wilderness and Time 107
Chapter 10	The Voice of God The Lord of Hosts 137

PART II

Chapter 11	My Beginning 157
Chapter 12	Back in the USA 167
Chapter 13	Stepping Out 177
Chapter 14	Skating Again 193

Introduction

The intention of this book is to bring to light evidence that suggests that there was a single primeval source of knowledge from prehistoric times from which sprang most of the religious systems of the world to this present day, and to identify what caused them to diverge from one another and form the different cultures that make up our world. Also to discover what the message of this knowledge is. It is possible this could be the genesis of history itself. The notion that history begins with religion is more than plausible. This primeval religious order has left us with a cosmic road map in the night sky, and memorials here on earth as a testimony to who they were for posterity's sake.

For those with the patience to follow through this work, I believe there is a gift of grace and insight as your reward at its completion. This insight will be waiting for as many of those who are willing to take to heart this information concerning these similarities. In my opinion these theological similarities are both uncanny and overwhelming. As a student of ancient cultures and religions, these similarities are impossible for me to ignore. Yet I am confident that many of the academic elite and the orthodox theologians alike will dismiss me outright. My intention is not to build a case for those who are looking for evidence of the lost continent of Atlantis, or is it to support the belief that extraterrestrials ie, aliens from another planet have come to earth to influence, or form early civilization.

I would like to take a moment to acknowledge Robert Baval and Adrian Gilbert for their research and work on the pyramids of Giza and the Sphinx. I would also like to mention in acknowledgment Professor of Geology Robert Schock of Boston University, and S.A. Nigosian, for his work done on Zoroastrianism. He is the author of "The Zoroastrian Faith, Traditions & Modern Research." Also the work of John Gibbons author of "The Decline and Fall of the Roman Empire." And the "Sky Map Pro 6" Astronomy Program, and Robert Burnham Jr. author of "Burnham's Celestial Handbook" along with both the Old and New Testaments of the Bible. It is from theses sources where I have drawn most of my reference material that I use in support of this presentation. I have studied the Old and New Testaments of the Bible for over 23 years, ever since God first revealed himself to me. With an unorthodox point of view, by some people's accounts, this along with my studies of ancient culture in general, I think has helped to enable me in pointing out the similarity of these cultures, and where these similarities have become differences, and hopefully be able to bridge the gulf of understanding between polytheistic and monotheistic applications of faith.

My goal is not to unify one with the other but rather to insight the readers' understanding to the possibility that both started with the same primary single source of knowledge, and then after time parted ways. For me this evidence of this single primary source of knowledge and its message is overwhelming, or at the very least, substantial enough to support my view. I feel this subject deserves to be studied and subsequently acknowledged.

I believe it will take three-dimensional thinking to grasp what is written here, along with a large dose of patience. The reader will be moving back and forth through time, and across cultural differences repeatedly on their journey through time and history. There will be heavy quotations from the Bible and other ancient documents that are necessary to make the connections of the many similarities between these faiths. I hope you find the journey as enlightening and fulfilling as I have.

PART I

CHAPTER 1

Jacob's Understanding

I will begin with a statement from the Old Testament. In Genesis chapter one verse fourteen, when God is creating the heavenly bodies. The author says:

> And God said let there be lights in the firmament of the heaven to divide the day from the night, and let them be for signs and for times for days and for years. Gen 1:14.

With a close inspection of this passage of scripture it can be assumed from its face value that the author of Genesis is implying that God created the stars as a means of keeping time; along with the sun and moon. If so, then the stars of heaven can be used as a tool, as a kind of celestial clock, for the maintenance of our place in time.

Also when the disciples of Jesus asked him, how they might know when and what would be the signs of the coming of the end of time; that Jesus had prophesied. Jesus told them:

> There shall be signs in the sun and the moon and in the stars; and On earth distress of nations with great perplexity; the sea and waves roaring. Luke 21:25

As with the statement in Genesis, this statement by Jesus of Nazareth tells there will be signs to be seen in the creation of the heavenly bodies that will testify to these coming events. This statement by Jesus has been nearly completely overlooked or shunned by most theologians of the western world. In another passage of the scriptures, in the gospel of Matthew Jesus is also hinting to this type of esoteric knowledge.

> Wherefore if they say to you behold, the Messiah is in the desert go not out with them or if they say behold he is in our inner chambers believe them not. For as the lightning (dawn) comes out of the east, and shines unto the west so also shall be the coming of the son of man. Mat 24:26-27

Again in the narratives of the birth of Jesus in the gospel of Matthew it states:

> Now when Jesus was born in Bethlehem of Judea, in the days of King Herod behold, there came wise men from the east to Jerusalem. Saying where is he that is born King of the Jews. For we have seen His star in the east, and have come to worship him. Mat 2:1-2

In some versions of the Bible it will say Astrologers in other versions it will say Magi, instead of wise men. The word Magi was a title of the priestly caste of the Zoroastrian faith from which we derive the word magician. Even as we derive the word wizard from the word wise; especially in the context it is used here. The order of Magi of the Zoroastrian religion has kept record with its observation of the stars and the sun and moon as have "Astrologers" as far back as history can record. Is it not possible this is the start of recorded time itself?

Equally interesting the Zoroastrian religion in its earliest stage of development was very similar to that of the Jewish religion and subsequently to the Christian faith as well. Subsequently may not be the appropriate word to use here at this time, but all three of these faiths believed in the following tenets:

> One Supreme Being
> The concept of angelic orders
> The concept of heaven
> The concept of hell
> The resurrection of the body and life everlasting
> Individual judgment
> The arrival of a coming Messiah
> (For Christians this is fulfilled in Jesus Christ)
> Cosmic events in the heavens at the time of the end of this epoch
> The final battle of Armageddon
> The millennium reign of the King of Righteousness

Yet even though these religions were all very similar with one another it is a startling statement in the gospel of Matthew that these Magi would seek out Jesus to worship him as their Messiah. Nationalism must have prompted major disagreements among their own peers.

The Zoroastrian religion is said to be a reform movement of a much older religion of the Middle East. According to Zoroastrian tradition, these reforms were initiated by the prophet Zoroaster. According to the classical historians such as Herodotus, Plutarch and Pliny the Elder, Zoroaster lived around 6,000 B.C. while the Islamic historians placed him around 600 B.C. Most modern historians accept this time frame as accurate.

Zoroaster's revelation and reform movement according to Zoroastrian history and tradition is as follows: Zoroaster was attending the celebration of the Spring Equinox, and while he was fulfilling his duties as priest, he was drawing water while in midstream of a river, as was the custom of their sacred ritual. Upon beginning his return to the river bank he saw a shining figure of an Archangel standing on the waters of the river. This Archangel is said to have brought Zoroaster into the presence of the five immortals of the glory of Ahura Mazda.

Ahura Mazda instructs Zoroaster in his principles of true faith. After these events Zoroaster enters into direct confrontation with his own priesthood, this conflict would last the rest of his life. During this time he denounces the excesses and shameless perversions instituted in the rites of his own religious priesthood that he also had taken part in, in the past. He calls for a return to Ahura Mazda's original concepts.

Now ostracized by his fellow priests, he is cast into prison for many years. The reforms he called for eventually begin to win converts and in time became an independent entity from its earlier counterpart. Yet both were priesthoods that employed astrological terminology; according to Zoroastrian tradition.

It is this earlier priesthood that archaeologist Dr. Selim Hassan believes made annual pilgrimages to Giza in Egypt, from as early as the beginning of the second millennium B.C.

The Great Sphinx in Giza of Egypt was a holy site to these Mesopotamians as well as to the Egyptians. Dr. Hassan excavated evidence of a colony near the Great Sphinx in Egypt of what he believed were these pilgrims from the ancient Assyrian's sacred city of Harran. Dr. Hassan identified these Semitic people as the Sabians.

The word Sabian is derived from the Egyptian tongue meaning "Star Worshipper". I believe that these Sabians and their religious order can be linked to the priesthood that Zoroaster strived to reform some two thousand years later. This can be accomplished through Zoroastrian traditions, and through their calendar systems. Both the Sabians and the Egyptians used the same calendar based on 360 days in a year plus five days to honor the five Neter Gods. Interestingly, the Zoroastrian calendar is also based on 360 days in a year, plus five days in honor of the five immortals that make up the Glory of Ahura Mazda. We are very fortunate that Zoroaster left this calendar system intact during his reforms. Also both the early Sabians and the ancient Egyptians' calendars are represented with symbols of the zodiac for each month of the year. This is also true of the Zoroastrian calendar as well.

Both the Sabians and the later Zoroastrians used the title of Magi. Also, the Sabians are supposed to have had received their sacred writings directly from Thoth-Hermes who was said to be the

Egyptian god of wisdom.

In these very early times the Egyptian and the Sabian religions, who Zoroaster later in history attempted to reform, had the comparable difference not much unlike the Roman Catholic and the Eastern Orthodox Churches of today.

The very interesting point in all of this is both the Egyptian and the Sabian-Zoroastrian calendars made exception to commemorate five days, in honor of the five Neter gods and the other in honor of the five immortals of Ahura Mazda.

A third occurring similarity that links all this to both the New Testament and Old Testament faiths of the Bible is first found in the book of the prophet Ezekiel. In the book of Ezekiel, Ezekiel has a vision while he is in captivity, by Nebuchadnezzar King of Babylon in the land of the Chaldeans, while at the river which was called Chebar in ancient times. God reveals his glory to Ezekiel. In the midst of this, Ezekiel sees four living creatures with one likened to a man sitting on a great throne within the center of the four living creatures. The complete first chapter of the book of Ezekiel is dedicated to this vision, thus the five.

The next example of this reoccurring similarity can be found in the Book of St. John's Revelation of Jesus Christ, also known as the Apocalypse. It is also the last book of the Bible. The Apostle John who received this revelation recounts his vision to paper in chapter 4 verses 6-9. He writes:

> Before the throne there was a sea of glass like unto crystal and in the midst of the throne and round about the throne were four creatures full of eyes before and behind. The first creature was like a lion and the second creature was like a calf, and the third creature had a face of a man, and the fourth creature was like a flying eagle: And the four creatures each had six wings and were full of eyes within: They never rested day or night always saying Holy Holy Holy LORD GOD ALMIGHTY which was and is and is to come. And these creatures gave glory and honor and thanks to him that sat on the throne who

lives for ever and ever. Rev 4:6-9.

Again we see in the midst of the glory of God the one and the four, making the five, as with Zoroaster's vision of God whom he called Ahura Mazda, so also with both Ezekiel and John, whom they knew as Yahweh.

Another interesting similarity is the Zoroastrian religion sees fire as the expression or essence of Ahura Mazda's nature. This is how God expressed himself to Moses; as Yahweh and his nature as fire, with the burning bush that was not consumed by the flames.

Also in the Gospel of Matthew, Jesus feeds the multitudes that had come to hear him speak. He feeds everyone that was present with <u>five</u> loaves of bread, and two fishes. When they collected the fragments that were left over they filled twelve baskets. Here is a concept to give some thought to. Fueling ones own existence without consuming creation, yet continuing! Possibly this is a subtle hint of the expression of the true nature of God.

Could these different people from different nations and faiths all commune with the same being? Even though Zoroaster was imprisoned by his peers, his reform movement finally caught hold in the Mead and Persian empires; even as it is recorded on wall carvings at their ancient capital of Persepolis.

It is at this time in history the Persians conquer the Babylonians some eight hundred to one thousand years after the time of Moses, this sets up the return of the captivity of Judah in Babylon to their home land and Jerusalem. As it is recorded in 2nd Chronicles Chpt. 36:22-23

> Now in the first year of Cyrus King of Persia that the word of the Lord spoken by Jeremiah might be fulfilled the LORD stirred up the spirit of Cyrus King of Persia that he made a proclamation throughout all His kingdom, and put it in writing saying: Thus says Cyrus King of Persia. All the kingdoms of the earth hath the Lord God of heaven given me. He hath charged me to build him a house in Jerusalem, which is in Judah. Who are there among you all his

people the Lord his God be with him then let them go up. Chronicles 36:22-23

It is no stretch to say that early Zoroastrian faith was akin to that of the captivity of Judah in Babylon. Why else would King Cyrus of Persia, ordain the return of the Jews to Judah and order the rebuilding of the temple in Jerusalem?

With a close inspection of the book of Ezekiel and the book of Daniel, if these two books were combined into one, they would have all the criteria met for the biography of Zoroaster's life even according to Zoroastrian tradition and history. The visions of Ezekiel and the visions that Daniel received, when combined together into one story, describe in detail the events and vision received by Zoroaster.

The times of these two prophets also correspond to the time frame in which Zoroaster lived according to modern historians. The geographic regions in which these events take place are also correct as well. Both time and place match, as does the combined accounts of Ezekiel and Daniel's experience with God, as with the Zoroastrian account of Zoroaster's experience with Ahura Mazda...

It is completely possible that the Zoroastrian movement was the result of the contact of the Persian people with the captivity of Judah with the defeat of the Babylonians, and the Zoroastrian epic of Zoroaster could be derived from these two biblical prophets when they are combined into one account. If this scenario was visa-versa the Magi would never have been watching for the Messiah's star among another people other than their own. This is another important aspect to keep in mind as well.

Can this be why the Magi mentioned in Matthew's account of Jesus' birth, came to Bethlehem to worship Jesus five hundred years later, a child not of their own people, as both their King and Messiah? These Magi were patrons of the kings of Persia! Their act of paying homage to Jesus, one not of their own people is astounding to say the least, except when one takes into consideration the information presented here so far. According to the gospel of Matthew, God guides these men and warns them, in dreams, not to return to Jerusalem, but to return to their own land another way.

These men of another religious order were in essence (by following God's guidance) of the same faith as the Hebrew patriarchs the difference was they were not under the Law.

The concept of God in the monotheistic sense was not exclusive of the Jewish or i.e. Hebrew peoples. To the contrary, this theological understanding permeated the entire region of the Middle East, from times far earlier in history than that of Moses at least according to the Scriptures. Even in and around Moses's time there are accounts that this was the case. The Egyptian Pharaoh Amenhotep IV, also known as Akhenaten who lived two to one hundred fifty years before the time of Moses also believed in the one God concept as his father before him. However there is sufficient evidence to support Akhenaten's concept of one supreme God was the result of the integrated contact with a Semitic people identified as the Hyksos or (Shepherd- Kings), who occupied the eastern part of the Nile delta. This had undoubtedly influenced Egypt even as it is recorded by the Ancient Egyptians in their own history. These Semitics migrated to Lower Egypt some three to four hundred years earlier and possibly even earlier than that. Never the less academic scholars enjoy expounding that Moses borrowed this concept of one God, from Akhenaten when most assuredly this concept was brought by these Semitic people to the Egyptian's centuries earlier.

Now the man Balaam is Moses's contemporary, he is one not of the chosen people of Israel coming out of Egypt; but rather he was from the mountains east of Mesopotamia in modern day Iran. This man also had direct communications with the same God as Moses did. This man Balaam at the hire of Balak, King of Moab, and the elders of the tribes of Midian, asked God to curse Moses and his people through Balaam. Balak and the elders of Midian must have also believed in the same God as well to have hired Balaam. Whom they regarded as a prophet and one who was blessed with his blessing was blessed, and one who was cursed with his curse was cursed. They must have revered him as great holy man of God, or they wouldn't have offered such a price if it were not so. But what comes out of the mouth of Balaam, to the horror of the King of Moab and the elders of Midian is a blessing and not a curse. He blesses Moses and the people of Israel. The whole episode of Balaam can be found in chapters twenty two thru twenty five in Numbers the fourth book of the Bible.

To elaborate on this fact that many different people and nations other than the nation of ancient Israel followed the consciousness of this one particular God, throughout the Middle East and beyond, we need to travel even further back in time, and examine three particular people. They are Abraham, Melchizedek, and Abimelech, here at approximately 700 years earlier than the time of Moses, around 1870 B.C. which is about mid-stream in time of the life of Abraham the patriarch of the nation of Israel. To whom God promises that from his lineage the Messiah of man is to be born. For this reason they are called the chosen people. It is also his great grandson Joseph in whom all the criteria is met for the Hyksos Kings or (Shepherd Kings) in Egypt. Abraham is told by God to leave his fathers house in the city of Harran. (The same city of the Ancient Sabians according to Dr. Hassan)

> Now the Lord said to Abraham: Depart from your country, and from the Place of your nativity, and from your father's house, to a land that I will Show you: and I will make of you a great people, I will bless you, and make your name great; and you shall be a blessing; and I will bless those, that bless you, and I will curse those that curse you; and in you shall all the families of the earth be blessed. So Abraham did as the lord had spoken to him; and Lot (his nephew) went with him; and Abraham was seventy-five years old when he departed from Harran. Genesis 12:1-4

The next of these three men is Melchizedek; he was the King of Salem a city of the Canaanites. Melchizedek was also the Priest of the Most High God, according to the book of Genesis. This Priest King blesses Abraham for his bravery and unselfishness for his part in a regional war, in which Abraham enters the conflict only to rescue his family members who are swept up in the conflict as innocent bystanders. In their deliverance Abraham refused the spoils of his victory when they are offered to him not even taking so much as a shoelace from his enemy for his own personal gain, he sought only the safe return and freedom of his family, for this he was blessed.

> And Melchizedek brought forth bread and wine; and he, was the Priest of the Most High God and he blessed Abraham saying Blessed be Abraham of the Most High God possessor of Heaven and Earth: and Blessed be the Most High God which has delivered your enemies into your hand. Gen. 14:18-20

The last of these three men is Abimelech. He is King of Gerar; one of the cities of Philistine. The accounts of his faith in the Most High God is found in the 20th chapter of Genesis particularly verses 3-5.

> But God came to Abimelech in a dream at night and said to him. Behold you are but a dead man, for the woman that you have taken Is another man wife. But Abimelech had not touched her yet. And he said LORD will you slay a righteous nation? Behold this Man said "She is my sister" and she herself said "He is my brother" In the innocence of my heart and purity of my hands have I done this. Gen 20: 3-5

All three of these men communicated with the same God, yet they were all of different peoples of different nations, speaking with and being spoken to by the same God. This in the middle of what is supposed to be a sea of polytheism. Many people within these different nations also held to a monotheistic concept even as in ancient Israel some held to polytheism. Although the majority of people, in these other nations most undoubtedly held with the polytheistic concept as the identifying characteristic of their nations, what seems to be emerging is two different applications of faith and belief. So this concept of monotheism as being exclusive to ancient Israel is a misconception even according to their own

Jacob's Understanding

sacred writing, in the Bible.

(I must interject here that I see a vast gulf between faith and belief. The two have many striking similarities, but yet they are poles apart from one another. The difference between faith and belief, or better put, the traditions of one's belief and faith are quite different but yet very subtle and will be discussed in later chapters.)

For now it is these numerous similarities that exist between the two that are to be examined. Some of which are just impossible to ignore, making seemingly outside possibilities more and more plausible. In support of this evidence that there is a single original source of knowledge from which nearly all religions of the ancient world originate from, to include the Gods of Greek mythology, and Egyptian mythology, along with the Middle East and most of Europe, and also to the Far East, thousands of years before recorded history began.

We now must consider what is present in all these cultures, and this is the Zodiac. It is present in one form or another world wide from prehistoric times. Yet never the less it is there, and it must be taken into consideration regardless of opinions or consequences. Now let us examine the twelve houses of the Zodiac. They are the twelve Constellations represented in the totality of time, in our own universe from the perspective of earth. They are a means of keeping track of time, with the sun and moon, even as it was mentioned in the opening statement of chapter one from this book; quoting from the book of Genesis. Also we will examine the twelve sons of the Hebrew patriarch Jacob, (the grandson of Abraham), and the significance of the number twelve to both. The number twelve is a sacred number but it is not completed or fulfilled until two more are present in its midst making fourteen. This is the number of complete totality, even as with Jacob and his wife with their son's make fourteen, even so with God the Father and, Jesus with his twelve Apostles.

If we look in greater detail at the prophetic blessing of Jacob to his sons in the waning days of his life on earth, as it is recorded in Genesis chapter 49, he (Jacob) tells each of his sons what will befall them in their latter days according to their nature's that they expressed while living here on earth. Also, he portrays their characteristics and mannerisms before them and blesses them accordingly. Astonishingly enough if we look at the twelve symbols that represent the twelve houses of the Zodiac with each symbol's attributes. Then compare this with the blessing of Jacob concerning his sons, and compare his characterization and attributes he ascribes to his twelve sons, you will find they are nearly identical, to those of the Zodiac. Reuben compares with Aquarius, Zebulon with Pisces, Simeon and Levi because of their wrath and deceit compare with Aries and Scorpio. Dan compares with Libra, Dan is the judge of his people, and Libra is denoted by a set of scales for justice. Joseph with Gemini for his two sons, Judah compares with Leo; this one is the most intriguing of all, and we will return to it in great detail later. The other five on all accounts compare closely as well. When taking these comparisons into account the evidence is beginning to mount that suggests the existence of this sky clock was known. It is my contention that Jacob knew of it, and understood the mechanics of it as the mechanics of heaven and that his destiny is also built into it as well. It is also clear he saw his sons as the stars or constellations of heaven as the very numerals of this clock in heaven. This is what the author of Genesis is implying; this can be plainly seen when Joseph tells a dream he had to his father and brothers in chapter 37 verses 9&10 of Genesis:

> And he dreamed yet another dream and Joseph told it to his brothers and He said behold I have dreamed another dream the Sun and Moon and The Eleven Stars were made to bowed down to me. When he told it to his father and to his brothers, his father rebuked him and said to him. What is this dream? Shall I and your mother and your brothers indeed come to bow down ourselves to the ground to you?
> Jacob Gen 37 : 9,10

Jacob also knew of the motion of the sun in its annual north south migration as another wheel. He knew that together these wheels are the mechanics of the cosmic clock. I will prove this. It is interesting to say the least, archaeologists working in the Qumran

Jacob's Understanding

excavations in the wilderness of Judea discovered along with the Dead Sea scrolls, a building at the center of the Essene's activity with a mosaic in its floor of what scholars agree is a mosaic of the zodiac. There have been other ancient mosaics of the zodiac discovered in other locations though out modern Israel. These mosaics have surprised and perplexed many scholars, and have raised many questions. Because the religion of ancient Israel was completely opposed to the practice of Astrology it was forbidden by both the Law of Moses and by the Prophets, but if it is a question of the application of the understanding of a more ancient knowledge, then these symbols that appear to be the Zodiac, and for the practice of astrology are in actuality the twelve sons of Jacob, as he described each of his sons, before he passed from this world.

Then this would give a completely different meaning and understanding to these mosaics.

Before continuing I must reiterate Jacob's (Israel's) last words concerning Simeon and Levi:

> Simeon and Levi are brethren their swords are weapons of violence In their habitations. Oh my soul come not thou into their secret: unto Their assembly, mine honor, be not thou united: Gen 49: 5-6

In proceeding further, a longer look is needed explaining Melchizedek who I mentioned earlier. In the New Testament, in the epistle to the Hebrews, the writer speaks of this Priest King Melchizedek of the book of Genesis, as being without father or mother without descendents having neither beginning nor ending. The writer of Hebrews likens this Melchizedek to the son of God, adding he is a priest continually forever. The writer of Hebrews must be referring to the Priesthood of Melchizedek, and not the man Melchizedek. In the same way as Jesus' statement to Peter "flesh and blood has not shown this to you but my Father in Heaven. Upon this rock I will build my church." It is this; being shown by revelation that is the rock on which his church is built. This is the meaning of being without father (flesh and blood) or mother without descendents having no beginning or ending in the epistle of Hebrews. If we are to take these passages in the epistle of Hebrews literally, rather than figuratively we must then ask why would King David attack Melchizedek's city of Salem? Then change its name to Jerusalem and then make this city the capital of Israel. Why would David's son Solomon build the temple and fill it with Levitical Priests, if Melchizedek the man was already there, and him having no end; why then would King David utter in the psalms?

> The Lord has sworn and will not repent, thou art a priest forever after the Order of Melchizedek. Psalms 110: 4

What was it that prompted King David to show this kind of

Jacob's Understanding

homage to this super priest that, one thousand years after his own time, King David would invoke his name? Rather than Aaron the High Priest of the Levitical Priesthood, of the tribe of Levi installed by Moses from within King David's own nation, which he was ruler of. If one considers the <u>"Order"</u> of Melchizedek as being without beginning and without end, a priesthood of the Most High God, which has always been here on earth since the earliest times of antiquity simply put before time began, in the same manner as Jesus acknowledged the confession of the Apostle Peter. Then King David's confession of faith is quantified with history.

It will be shown that this priesthood of Melchizedek is the architect of the Great Sphinx of Egypt. It will be shown that the Egyptian religion is an off-shoot of this priesthood. Also, where and how, and why they parted company. It will be shown that this "Order" of Melchizedek were astronomers par excellence guided by God, above and beyond anything that the astrologers of the Egyptian priesthoods of Heleopolis and On could even begin to comprehend, the knowledge that the Order of Melchizedek possessed came by interjection of (revelation) and not by observation of the stars. Some of this evidence has already been hinted to, and can partly be seen in the earlier pages of this book, with the complete understanding of the stars and constellations that Jacob (Israel) possessed. Also I will show a fraternity of people with those who have already been mentioned, that will include Daniel, Isaiah, and Ezekiel, along with the Apostles of Jesus and his disciples, with Jesus of Nazareth at the head of this fraternity. A fraternity whose belief are manifested by faith in the "Living Voice" of the Most High God, as he spoke to them in the moment, as they walked in response to the hearing of his voice. Also, I will expound on the differences between mythology and prophecy and show the unequivocal difference between the two. We will discover the riddle of the Great Sphinx of Giza and examine the most recent geological evidence to its date of construction as well.

This geological evidence begins in the early 1960's by a Mathematician and Egyptologist, R.A. Schwaller de Lubicz. Schwaller's Publication of (Sacred Science) comments: ... "If the single fact of the water erosion of the Sphinx could be confirmed it would in itself overthrow all accepted chronologies of the history of civilization; it would force a drastic re-evaluation of assumption of 'progress' – the assumption upon which the whole of modern education is based. It would be difficult to find a single, simpler question with graver implication..."In 1989 John Anthony West, an American researcher, collaborated with Professor Robert Schock of Boston University they conducted geological surveys with the permission of the Egyptian Antiquities Organization in Cairo. The conclusion of their work was, from the evidence of water erosion on the Sphinx' back and on the 200 ton limestone blocks in the Sphinx temple they dated these structures conservatively between 7000 to 4000 B.C. This is 1500 to 4500 years earlier than Egyptologists believe, but some academics say this is still inconclusive. One way or the other, this evidence has split the academic community. With geologists and paleo-climatologists including the Geological Society of America on the one hand and the orthodox Egyptologists on the other, with a growing amount of archaeologists split on this issue. Some are suggesting an advanced civilization of unidentified origin prior to the Egyptian culture is responsible for the construction of the Sphinx. I believe there is sufficient evidence to support such a statement; not just because of the geological evidence alone, but also from the cultural evidence as well. Some has already begun to surface in the similarities presented so far, with mounting evidence to come. Along with geographical evidence, mathematical, linguistic evidence and astronomical evidence, that are all converging simultaneously to testify to who the true architects of the Great Sphinx are. If so, what is the message of this pre-Egyptian culture and how does it tie into the people we have spoken of so far and how does this affect you?

CHAPTER 2

The Coming Promise

The next of these similarities are quite interesting but very controversial and somewhat complicated in making these connections at the start. I ask you the reader not to assume where this is going, but to follow through so you will know for fact rather than making assumptions of what I am presenting, because many times in life things are not as they first appear.

In the study of Egyptian mythology, the Egyptian god of resurrection is Osiris. Isis is his wife and sister. She is the queen of heaven. The child of their union is Horus he is the God king, the reunifier of the two lands, and the restorer of order. The legends of these deities are intricate and complex. Coalescing deities into composite gods, in order to harmonize their mythological lives, with what the Ancient Egyptian Astronomer Priests saw as the mechanics of the heavens. They corroborated these concepts with the houses of the Zodiac. Their purpose was to faithfully reenact the legendary deeds of these Gods in the cosmos. All this was done to assist the Egyptian royalty in their journey to the afterlife. These deities were of the utmost importance to the Ancient Egyptians. Their concern was not if they would achieve resurrection, but rather what quality of life they would have upon entering into it.

First a closer inspection is needed at Osiris and his heavenly counterpart the constellation of Orion, along with Orion's companion star Sirius that follows closely behind Orion through the night sky.

This star Sirius's counterpart in Egyptian mythology is Isis. In this mythology Osiris is murdered by his brother Seth, and then is resurrected with the help of Isis by joining in union with Osiris and receiving his seed. This is in the Egyptian religion their highest of holy days. It is commemorated as Osiris having fully risen. This union brings forth Horus who restores the order that was lost by the murder of his father, and again reunifies the two lands.

For now, it is this moment of union of Osiris and Isis and their celestial counterpart Orion and Sirius in the night sky we are most concerned with. In Astronomy the rising of Orion in the eastern sky is not considered complete or "fully risen" until the star Sirius can be seen on the eastern horizon as well, just before dawn immediately followed by the rising of the Sun when both Orion and Sirius disappear in the presence of the morning Sun. This happened in Ancient times annually just about the time of the summer solstice.

This also coincided with the annual flooding of the Nile River. The flooding of the Nile brought new life to Egypt each year, fertilizing the delta and its flood planes. The ancients attributed this annual flood to Osiris having fully risen and bestowing resurrecting life to the whole of Egypt.

To the Christian, Jesus Christ is the Lord of the resurrection of life. Also the church is his bride, essentially making the church that is to say the true church those that are believers in God and Jesus Christ as a living person in them, these are the Queen of Heaven.

Also in comparison, Jesus of Nazareth is murdered by the Jewish High priest his brethren, on what the Jewish faith calls Passover. To the follower of Jesus this is the ultimate Passover. Jesus is their sacrificial Lamb of God the Messiah.

On this day he dies by crucifixion. That coming Sunday, Easter Sunday as it is called; he is raised from the dead, as it is recorded in the Gospels. The Angels roll away the stone that had covered the entrance of his tomb. Later on that same morning a disciple named Mary Magdalene came with spices to anoint the dead body of her master. But she found his tomb empty. Then seeing a man she thought to be the caretaker of the cemetery, she asked him, "Where have they laid my master's body." It is then and only when Jesus

The Coming Promise

calls her by name, she can recognize him, and she moves to embrace him. But Jesus says: "Touch me not for I am not yet ascended to my Father." John 21:17.

This statement by Jesus: Touch me not for I am not yet ascended to my Father, is of great significance!

Jesus tarries on earth for some forty days or so after his crucifixion expounding the Kingdom of God to his disciples. Then Jesus ascended into heaven in the presence of his disciples. Later that coming week when the feast of Pentecost was full, which is the 50th day after Passover, his disciples were together in one accord waiting on the promise that Jesus had made to them "For when I go to my father and your father I will send you the Holy Ghost." Then suddenly, there came the sound of mighty wind and tongues of fire rested on all that were in the room, and they were filled with the Holy Ghost and power. Even as it was recorded in the book of Acts, they began to speak in other languages as the Holy Spirit gave them utterance. They spoke in the tongue of the Parthians and Meads that is to say the two dialects of the Persian language. Others spoke in the language of the Elamite, and all the dialects of Mesopotamia. While others spoke in the tongue of Cappdoccia and Pontus and of Asia also of Phrygia Egypt and Rome, Crete and Arabia.

According to the chronicler of the Book of Acts, Jerusalem was filled with people from all over the known world and every man heard the same message in his own tongue, and that day alone three thousand souls accepted the message of the Holy Spirit each person, man and woman, hearing it in their native tongue. In a moment's time flooding the known world with the same message, Jesus of Nazareth as the foretold Messiah of all the prophets.

If we take into consideration all the differences in the different calendar systems used at this time, this event takes place precisely at the same time as the astronomical event of Orion having fully risen. Pentecost can occur in the same time frame because of the great variances in the Lunar calendars used to designate the day of the Passover thus fifty days later is Pentecost. This flood of the Holy Spirit happens only after Jesus is fully risen to the right hand of the Father to receive all power in heaven, and is established as not only the Lamb of God, but also as the "Lion of the tribe of

Judah". This flooding of the Holy Ghost and the flooding of the Nile River both happened on the same day, both signifying the power of the resurrection.

In the Hebrew feast of Pentecost, the Feast of First Fruits as it is called, is when the first blade of barley comes forth to ripen, and with the Christian Pentecost concerning Jesus Christ, it is the completion and establishment of his resurrection by the coming of the Holy Ghost. Are these feasts borrowed from the Ancient Egyptians? Or! Are they all linked to a single source of knowledge in the distant past? Had the Ancient Egyptians lost the meaning of this event and unwittingly celebrating the union of Christ and the church, with the bestowed gift of the Holy Ghost, in the coming future with their observance of the union of Osiris and Isis and Orion and Sirius from their mythology

King David proclaims in Psalm 19:1: The heavens declare the glory of God, and the firmament shows his handiwork. If this is so, the Gospel of Jesus of Nazareth, the Christ must be displayed in the night sky. If Jesus is the glory of God, I believe this is the case.

Many skeptics at this point are dismissing me as a blaspheming heretic by now, because of the connections I have espoused so far. I ask only that they be not hasty in their judgment and make righteous judgment. If they will bear with me it will be shown, both geographically and astronomically in the coming chapters that these intriguing similarities with Jesus Christ fully rising and Osiris fully rising are neither borrowed one from the other nor are they coincidental.

On the contrary many of the stories from Egyptian, Greek and Babylonian mythology show striking similarities with both the Old and New Testaments. Including other than the Jesus, and Osiris connection and the church and Isis connections, for instance. The occasion when Moses makes a staff with brazen serpents intertwined upon it for the healing of snake bit victims, in the wilderness during Israel's sojourn to the Promised Land. This is reminiscent of the Greek God of healing, symbolized by serpents intertwined around a staff. This is the symbol of Medicine even to this day. It is called the caduceus of Hermes and Hermes is the Greek version of Thoth the Egyptian God of wisdom. This brings us to the story of the dueling serpents, when Moses and Aaron's serpent, and the high priest of Egypt and his serpent fight, and Moses's serpent devours the Egyptian's serpent signifying who possessed the greater wisdom and power.

Another example; take for instance the stories of Zeus and the other gods coming out of heaven and taking the women of earth to produce the demigods such as Hercules, Perceus and others {I will not attempt to name them all} from Greek mythology. Compare this with an unusual passage in Genesis 6:1-4, but particularly verse four in Genesis it states: that the sons of God had union with the daughters of men and they produced "mighty men which were of old, men of renown." To be renown, one's reputation must be spread abroad. But there is no mention of any of these men of renown in Genesis so how could they be renown? By what criteria are they renowned who could the author of Genesis be writing about? Or is this a shadow of the Hercules' and Perceus' of mythology and such? Such is endless confusion. Never the less these stories run parallel through history and the cultures. It is this very babble that the event of tongues on Pentecost signified the abrogation of. The event of Pentecost is; the very antithesis of what took place at the Tower of Babble from whence come all the varying languages and subsequent religions according to the Bible.

What we will do is look at the heavens with an astronomical point of view to see the science of the mechanics of the heavens and reflect on what the stars in the night sky are saying every day. How is it that the heavens declare the glory of God and the firmament shows his handiwork? Or was King David just trying to flatter the Almighty? Or was the Almighty prophesying to us through King David?

CHAPTER 3

The Stars of Heaven

The mechanical process that is continually in motion dictating the movement of the stars and constellations through the heavens in astronomical terms is called precession. It is by this phenomenon of precession that the constellations can be plotted year by year, century by century, and millennium by millennium across the night sky. When we look toward the eastern horizon of the sky these constellations such as Leo and Orion in particular, appear to be moving northward against the eastern horizon at a average rate of one degree every 72 years, over the course of 12,960 years. Then they shift and move southward for 12,960 years. Why? Because of a slow wobble in the earth's axis. This wobble takes 25,920 years to complete one cycle.

At its transitional points from ascent to descent these constellations slow dramatically, at least to the naked eye with respect to their movement through the night sky, they appear to move not much more than one degree over one thousand years. This movement through the heavens is the Great Wheel or Great Cycle. It is divided into twelve stations or twelve houses, known to astronomers as the twelve houses of the Zodiac. Each station or house is a time of 2,160 years 2,160 years x 6 = 12,960 years in ascent and 2,160 x 6 = 12,960 in their descent. So then when added together there are 25,920 years all told. It is the same principle as the clock in your kitchen. This is the mechanics of the great wheel of the cosmic clock. Today's modern astronomers define one cycle of this wheel as one stellar year. It is no stretch that the ancients would have called any age of the houses of the Zodiac simply a "time."

The earth is now entering into the very highest point of this precessional movement, the transition from ascent to descent. This point is the 25,920 year marker of the completion of one stellar year or one great cycle. For the next one thousand years the constellations and the stars will seemingly come to a stand-still as they are viewed from earth in their precessional movement. They will move less than one degree from where they are today for the next one thousand years. Time, in the precessional sense will have stopped for the next one thousand years, then they will resume in descent, this is the science of Astronomy. Every modern astronomer in the world today will verify this mechanical event of the heavens is a fact without exception.

This celestial event is also prophesied in the Bible 2,700 years ago in exact description and detail by the prophet Isaiah, then again two hundred years later by the prophet Daniel, then by the Apostle John nearly two thousand years ago, each adding portions of their descriptions of the details of this event. All three of these prophets foretold this very same event with exacting descriptions in their own words. Even as to how it would appear to people here on earth and this can be seen by all that are astute enough to look for it, for themselves. We will look at each of these prophets, and what they foretold in detail, and who they were as individuals.

This will reveal a pattern that is beginning to emerge which will show a benign relationship with astronomy and prophecy, even though the terminology it was presented in was basically astrological.

We will begin with the prophet Daniel. When King Nebuchadnezzar, King of Babylon, sacked and destroyed Jerusalem in the year 605 B.C. he gave orders to one of his captains that read as follows: The King spoke to Ashpenaz the Master of his eunuchs that he should bring certain of the children of Israel and of the King's seed and princes thereof. Men in whom was no blemish of reputation and well favored and skillful in all wisdom and cunning in knowledge with the understanding of science. They that would have the ability to serve in the King's palace in whom they might teach the learning and tongue of the Chaldeans. These were in preparation for three years to serve the King. Among them was Daniel. At the end of three years they were brought before King Nebuchadnezzar and their knowledge was tested. In the matters of wisdom and understanding of science, the King found Daniel's knowledge surpassed all his magicians and astrologers in these matters. In time King Nebuchadnezzar had a disturbing dream, and there were none among his own court magicians and astrologers that could tell him his dream or its meaning and the King was enraged at their inabilities. They were all to be put to death. Daniel not yet at the King's court hears of the death sentence from a fellow servant and goes before the King to ask for time. The King grants his request. Daniel returns later with the dream and its interpretation. King Nebuchadnezzar rewarded him with the promotion to governor of all the wizards, magicians and astrologers of Babylon. This is a condensed and paraphrased version of Daniel chapters 1, 2, 3.

Daniel's ability to surpass these magicians and astrologers in the understanding of their own wisdom and science was accomplished without offending his God or betraying his own faith. How did he do this? We return to a word I have used often so far, and this is application. I believe this exemplifies considerable evidence that a universal knowledge of the heavens did exist, and it came down to interpreting what God had put in motion by beholding either the creation or the Creator. God revealed these esoteric principles of ancient knowledge to Daniel because of the integrity of his heart with the guidance of the Holy Spirit. He Daniel acknowledged the Creator of creation as the conductor of this slow train coming, and not the mechanical train. This is how Daniel accomplished this feat.

The following is a prophecy given to Daniel concerning the astronomical event that is mentioned on page 33 of this book, when the earth begins its transitional wobble. The events spoken of in this prophecy are identical to the events spoken of by Isaiah and John in their prophecies. Both Isaiah and John go further and give a detailed account and description of this transitional wobble and describe the condition of the earth when this is to take place. They are all prophesying the same event. Daniel reads as follows:

At that time Michael shall stand up. The great prince which stands for the children of your people: and there shall be a time of trouble, such as never was since there were nations throughout all of time: and at that time your people shall be delivered every one that shall be found written in the book: and many of them that sleep in the dust of the earth shall awake some to everlasting life and some to shame and everlasting contempt. But they that be wise shall shine as the brightness of the firmament and they that turn many to righteousness as the stars forever and ever. But thou O Daniel shut up the words and seal the book, even to the time of the end: many shall run to and fro and knowledge shall be increased. Then I Daniel looked and behold there stood two other, the one on this side of the riverbank and the other on that side of the riverbank. And one said to the man clothed in linen which was standing upon the waters of the river. How long shall it be to the end of these wonders. I heard the man clothed in linen, which was upon the waters of the river, when he held up his right hand and his left hand unto heaven, and swore by him that lived for ever that it shall be for a times time and a half; and when he shall have accomplished to scatter the power of the holy people all these things shall be finished.

I heard but I understood not: then said I, oh my LORD what shall be the end of these things? But he said to me. Go the way Daniel; for The words are closed up and sealed till the time of the end.
Daniel 12:1-9.

If you will recall, a "time" in astrological terminology is the time it takes for an age to pass from one house of the zodiac to the next, which is 2,160 years, and a half a time would be another 1,080 totaling 3,240 years.

Daniel received this vision in the year circa 536 B.C. If a time's time is measured by the time of the passing from one house of the zodiac to another and then add another half again, it is 3,240 years which brings us to the year 2714 A.D.

This time of 2714 A.D. brings the earth into the beginning of the second half of the precessional transition just after the very apex of the wobble of this astronomical event. It is here when this slow wobble makes its subtle change of direction that brings us to the prophecy spoken by Isaiah in the approximate year 732 B.C. who first received this vision Isaiah reads as follows:

> The earth shall reel to and fro like a drunkard, and shall be removed like a cottage(Station): and the transgression there of shall be heavy upon all the earth: and it shall fall and will not rise again. It shall come to pass in that day, that the Lord shall punish the host of the high ones that are in places of power, and the kings (rulers) of the land upon the earth. They shall all be gathered together as criminals are gathered in the prison, and shall be shut in the dungeon. After many days they shall be visited.
>
> Than shall the moon by confounded, and the sun shall be ashamed, when the LORD of hosts shall reign in Mount Zion, and in Jerusalem, and before his ancients of the glorious. Isaiah Chapter 24:20-23.

If this criterion of calculation is used from the moment Isaiah received this vision, then his vision of the earth wobbling to and fro like a drunkard happens at the same time as the transitional wobble of the earth's axis at 2450 A.D., this is at the very apex of this astronomical event.

Both of these prophet's prophecies speak of the coming end of this world's governments, in conjunction with the beginning of the kingdom of God on earth, also with the coming judgment of the nations.

The prophetic event of the earth reeling to and fro like a drunkard in comparison with the astronomical event of the precessional transition of the wobble from ascent to decent is a remarkably accurate description of this event. Now if we use the time period of the zodiac as the time frame of calculation of the prophet Daniel's time's time and half a time, then this time period is the correct interpretation, and these events are one and the same.

John's description of the event of this transitional wobble of the earth's axis is wonderfully unique, as the precessional movement is towards north for 12,960 years then south for the same amount of time. When one is looking at the eastern horizon the sky will be rolling back in the direction it had come like opening and then rolling up a scroll. John also makes mention Michael John's vision in Revelations 6:14 states:

> The heaven departed as a scroll when it is rolled together; and every mountain and island were moved out of their places

This is a perfect description of this event and also speaks of every thing being moved out of its place the same as Isaiah's reference to the (cottages) or station being moved out of their place.

Is this just a coincidence? Or is modern man only slowly coming to the astronomical knowledge that the ancients possessed of the heavens? This that God has always professed to have created, (the heavens proclaim the glory of God and the firmament shows the work of his hands. Ps 19:1.) Now what of Daniel's and Isaiah's messages concerning this transitional wobble of the earth's axis? Is the timing from Daniel's prophecy and the description of the wobble in Isaiah's and John's prophecies of this astronomical event, just a good guess? Come on! The time linked to the described event with such accuracy! What then, if not a good guess and not a coincidence? It leaves only two other possible conclusions. One an interjection of a supreme knowledge as these men claim, or two, there would have to have been astronomers here on earth keeping detailed records for at least one thousand years before the last wobble of the earth's axis at 10,500 B.C. This is what would have to have been done to even know that any wobble in the earth's axis had even taken place. But the problem with this is, at this time in our pre-history around 11,500 B.C. the academics insisted mankind was not much more than pack hunters and gatherers. With only the most rudimentary use of tools and completely incapable of keeping such detailed astronomical records without the use of a sophisticated numbering system. Then, one might say, they accomplished this feat through oral tradition. Think about it, if that was the case then for them to know that this astronomical event was not a one time phenomenon in 10,500 B.C. in their night skies and that this event would repeat itself every 12,960 years as correctly predicted by Daniel, Isaiah and John in the year 2450 A.D. These presumed predecessors of Daniel, Isaiah and John would have had to witness the complete cycle at least once before, to have even known that this event in 10,500 B.C. was not a one time event, but rather a repeating cycle. This would place mankind at a minimum 24,000 B.C. with a capacity of keeping detailed records and implementing a sophisticated numbering system as to accurately forecast the time of the next two transitional wobbles of the earth axis. This would be completely impossible without a sophisticated writing and numbering system. Yet academics and evolutionists contend mankind was communicating at this time 24,000 B.C. with nothing more than simple grunts; and these people are going to do what it takes modern man's most sophisticated computer programs to do today! This leaves only one conclusion the interjection of supreme knowledge.

The ancient Egyptians called the time of the 10,500 B.C. precessional transition (the wobble) the Zep Tepti (the first time) and there is no indication of any knowledge on their part that the wobble even existed only that 10,500 B.C. was the beginning of time. Subsequently they had no idea that this astronomical event would repeat itself 12,960 years later around 2450 A.D. and no such event is mentioned in the whole of Egyptian liturgy.

Now the fact that these three Hebrew prophets did foretell the coming of this event in light that the most ancient form of Semitic languages like that of the city of Harran, from where Abraham came from had an alphabet that consisted of 24 consonants and 2 vowels, one vowel representing the male and one representing the female. 26 letters in all; much like our alphabet of today, thousands of years before King David recites his Psalm.

> Psalm 90:4 For a thousand years in thy sight is as yesterday.

This twenty six character alphabet from alpha to omega, A to Z, is for the acknowledgment of the 26,000 year cycle. It is also an affirmation of Jesus Christ in the book of Revelation "I am the Alpha and Omega." This is left to our posterity as a testimony of those who knew. Again look at another of King David's Psalms.

> Psalm 110:3-4 The people shall be willing in the day of power, in the beauty of holiness from the womb of morning: thou have the dew of youth. The LORD has sworn, and will not repent thou are a priest forever after the order of Melchizedek.

I am here to tell you that the priesthood of Melchizedek is the architect of the Sphinx at Giza in Egypt, and this observatory in itself could have been placed no where else on the earth. It is only here where it is today, that all these alignments of heaven and earth converge, only at this one single point on earth tied to Salem the city of Melchizedek. This will be demonstrated before you and unfolded in the following pages. This priesthood of Melchizedek was not looking backward in time like that of the Egyptian priesthood at Memphis, who were totally absorbed with the past, the Zep Tepi. Rather to the contrary, they of the priesthood of Melchizedek look to the future to the Omega as well as the Alpha, with their emphasis on coming events prophetically speaking with history as its witness, even as history unfolded itself. This is in sharp contrast to what later became the priesthood of Egypt at Memphis and Heleopolis. They interpreted the limited knowledge they had retained from the past turning it into a mythological application, as they looked backward in time to connect themselves and their nation and Pharaoh to God's Inheritance. Looking back is the definition of the word religion in itself. The Order of Melchizedek has the far greater astronomical accuracy in its understandings of the workings of alpha and omega; far more than what the Egyptians could even start to comprehend, they looked forward.

The Stars of Heaven

This leaves the building of the Sphinx complex to the order of Melchizedek at a time when the world was one people. Far before the fourth Dynasty of Egypt that is credited with its construction.

Now concerning John's witness of Jesus Christ and its connection with the constellation of Orion, John's witness in Revelation 1:8

> I am Alpha and Omega the beginning and the ending
> says the LORD which is and which was and which
> is to come the Almighty.

It is this connection that will be demonstrated first. Now in this, the last time when the astronomical event of the precessional wobble is about to commence, the constellation of Orion is nearly exactly where it was 25,920 years ago, at the beginning of this time cycle. Directly east of the Great Sphinx in Egypt on the eastern horizon, it will be the beginning of a new 25,920 year cycle in less than 400 years.

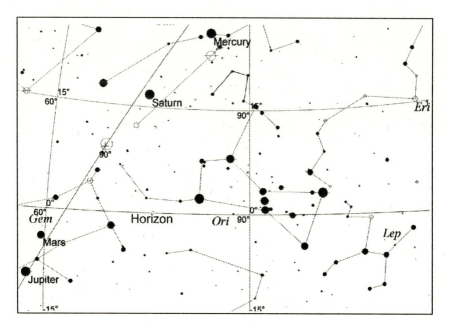

Fig. 2. Orion at 6:44 21st June 2002 A.D. and 23,470 B.C. viewed from the Great Sphinx.

So astronomically speaking one can say Orion represents Alpha and Omega. But how does that pertain to Jesus Christ, another might say? According to the Gospels Jesus rises on the third day after he is condemned to death by the Sanhedrin.

Astronomically speaking, Orion rises in three days as well. This takes place with Orion in conjunction with the sunrise around the beginning of summer very near the solstice.

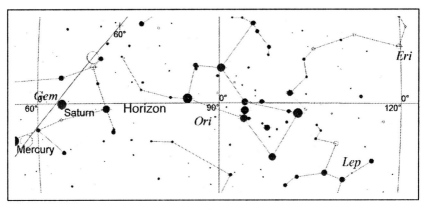

Time 04:21 18 June 33 A.D.

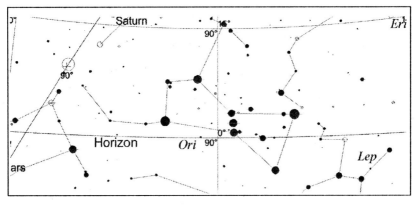

Time 04:21 21st June 33 A.D.

It is a three day rising period for the constellation of Orion, from out of the earth, when viewed by looking towards the eastern horizon, it is also three days until Jesus rises from the earth after they had arrested him and had condemned him to death. For it is at the moment of his betrayal that Jesus is in the hands of the heart of the earth. The constellation of Orion is representative of Jesus as the Lamb of God, and this is only the beginnings of this connection.

Another intriguing fact with these similarities is the two accounts found in the very early pages of the book of Genesis, the first book of the Bible and the ancient Egyptian liturgies.

Seth, in the Ancient Egyptian mythology is the brother of Osiris and Seth is sometimes depicted as a serpent. Seth becomes envious of his brother's Osiris' kingdom that Osiris had established on earth. Seth with the help of seventy two conspirators murders his brother Osiris by drowning him and seized his kingdom. Then Isis, Osiris' wife, finds her husband and joined with him as he was fading and conceived a son. In the Egyptian mythologies this is Horus, who in the due course of time reestablishes his father's kingdom.

Now the biblical Seth is the third son of Adam and Eve. Cain, their first son, murdered Abel their second son. God in his displeasure curses Cain for his act of violence and envy and sends Cain away cursed as a vagabond upon the face of the earth. Cain established himself in Nod to the east of Eden.

In time Adam again goes into his wife and Eve conceives, and Seth is born. It is this lineage through Seth that Noah is born who survives the flood and his offspring repopulate the earth.

It is from this line of Seth that the redeemer promised to Adam and Eve is to come. This redeemer is to be the one who reestablishes the union of God and man and restores what was interrupted by the serpent's beguilement of Adam and Eve. It is this lineage that the Bible so meticulously records from Seth to Noah, from Noah to Abraham, from Abraham to Isaac, from Isaac to Jacob (Israel the nation), and Moses and the law. By this was the nation of Israel defined as a people. As they that are under the Law of the Most High God.

To this people and this people alone could the redeemer be born. To this people is Jesus of Nazareth born. It is this man who tells the people that the Kingdom of God is at hand and the redemption of the beguilement of the serpent is accomplished. For all those who believe his message and believe that he is sent by God as the Redeemer and he himself is to be the price to be paid for this redemption as foretold by the prophets.

Now those in power with the Levitical priesthood established by Moses, it is their authority that is now threatened by this new teacher. In that he supercedes the Law of Moses with his teaching and yet he himself complies with and fulfills all the Law. But He is continuously breaking with the authority's idea of the Law by breaking their established traditions of the same.

As Jesus' following grows the authorities frustration grows as well, leading them to their decision that Jesus of Nazareth must die in order to save the identity of the nation. In that the nation's identity is in following the Law of Moses according to their traditions.

This, rather than the voice of God as Jesus of Nazareth proclaimed, and as Abraham to whom this promise is confirmed by faith also followed the voice of God in the same manner. They bring Jesus before the Sanhedrin under the charge of blaspheme and they condemned Jesus to die because he claimed to be the son of God.

This all takes place, historically speaking, approximately seventy two generations after the time of Moses. If one reckons a common generation to be around sixteen years. But if this reckoning is just a little too vague, put it aside for now.

In the book of Numbers of the Bible and the Mishna the book of established codes interpreting the Law of Moses, the Sanhedrin was made up of one and seventy persons. These are the number of the conspirators of Jesus of Nazareth's murder for there is no law that forbade anyone to claim... "God is my Father."

But the number is still one short to match with the number of conspirators with Seth in the murder of Osiris. But add one more for Judas Iscariot the Apostle that betrayed Jesus and you have the number of the conspirators as seventy two. Here is another intriguing connection between the Egyptian mythology and the death of Osiris and the prophecy of the coming death of Jesus Christ. Osiris is drowned by Seth, and Jesus is crucified at the insistence of the Sanhedrin his brethren, by the hands of Romans.

Death by crucifixion is actually a very slow form of drowning.

The lungs fill up with fluids and the victim dies by drowning. This is why both water and blood came from the stab wound Jesus received in his side when the Roman soldier pierced him with his spear after Jesus had already died, as it is recorded in the Gospel of John:

> But when they came to Jesus and saw that he was dead already they did not brake his legs but one of the soldiers with a spear pierced his side and forthwith came there out blood and water and he that saw does bare record and this record is true: and he knows that he says the truth: that ye might believe.
> St John 20: 33-35

This issuing of water and blood from Jesus' pierced lung was no supernatural miracle, but the evidence that he died from drowning. With the many executions done by the Romans in this manner, this was probably the way they checked every execution to see if their gruesome job had been completed. Malice may have never been that Roman soldier's motive at all.

So, as far as lineage goes, Seth historically did murder his brethren with seventy two accomplices by drowning him. To the ancient Egyptians this happened in the past with their mythological Osiris and by this, they the Egyptians, claimed their divinity with the Gods. From the viewpoint of the Order of Melchizedek, this was an oncoming event, culminating in the future that this redeemer's lineage would come from Seth and be murdered by the same, as it was played out with the life and death of Jesus Christ and his resurrection. Two thousand to three thousand years after the mythological story of Seth and Osiris. This is the time when Jesus fulfills his destiny as the Lamb of God two thousand years ago.

Now as it has been mentioned in the earlier pages, the connection of Isis being reminiscent of the star Sirius (and as the astral representation of the Church and as the Queen of Heaven), and the similarity with the summer solstice observances of Sirius and the Church's moment with Pentecost are uncannily similar. We will now discuss in greater detail.

Is the star Sirius the heavenly representation of the bride of Christ? We have seen unique knowledge that suggests the constellation of Orion as the celestial representation of the person of Jesus of Nazareth (the Lamb of God). How does Sirius then do the same other than following Orion through the night sky? What other evidence is there other than just the timing of Pentecost and the summer solstice observance of Isis and Sirius, and the flooding of the Nile and the flooding of the Gospel of Jesus Christ with the event of tongues at Pentecost?

At the time of the Roman Empire, and into antiquity, all astronomers describing Sirius described it as a great red star and not the brilliant white star that we see today. It is without question that this star has undergone the radical change from a red giant to a white dwarf seemingly overnight in astronomical terms. As close as Sirius B is to earth, as a red giant it must have been spectacular, even today as a white star, Sirius A, is the brightest star in the night sky. The question is how big would Sirius B have appeared as a red giant in the night sky 2,000 years ago? If this is the case it would have been easily the largest star in the night sky coupled with the brightest star in the night sky and without a doubt seen by the naked eye, as Sirius A orbited around Sirius B every fiftieth year on the backdrop of this red giant.

If is the case, Sirius B as a great red giant would explain why in the first century B.C. Cicero described Sirius as a ruddy blaze of fire. Even earlier Homer described Sirius as gleaming like the copper shield of Achilles. Ptolemy calls Sirius "the ruddy dog-star in that it followed Orion though the night sky" and Seneca at the time of Nero "Sirius is redder than Mars where Jupiter is not red at all."

This would also explain the mystery of the Dogon tribe of Mali in West Africa possessing the knowledge of these companion stars for millennia before Alvan G. Clark using an 18 ½ inch refracting telescope in January of 1862 was credited with the discovery of Sirius B the white dwarf. What would be very interesting to me is the celebration that accompanied the event of Sirius B completing its orbit around Sirius in its fifty year cycle.

Does this tribe the Dogon, forgive their debtors, and free their bond servants at this time; in how many ways does their celebration resemble the fifty year celebration of Jubilee practiced by Ancient Israel?

The Star of David which is the national symbol of Israel today; and of King David's time as well, is two intermingled triangles or pyramids.

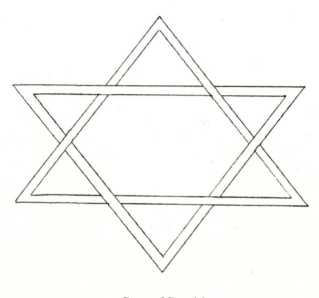

Star of David

This denotes two separate entities in perpetual motion around one another in essence becoming one. Combining this with the feast of Jubilee which is a feast of the whole nation, rather than one centered at the temple, strongly suggests that Ancient Judah saw itself as the star Sirius. While the Ancient Egyptian saw this star as the Goddess Isis, wife of Osiris (Orion).

It must be remembered that in ancient times this star was a red giant and not the stellar white as it is today. One particularly interesting fact is the word "Adam" means ruddy, flushed or red this word ruddy is the common descriptive for Sirius by these early Astronomers.

In the chronicles of the first book of the Bible in Genesis, God is said to have put Adam into a deep sleep and removed one of his ribs, and made him Eve. From out of the side of Adam came Eve: and the two became one flesh. Again this is denoted with two intermingled pyramids representing body, soul, and spirit together to make the Star of David represented in heaven by Sirius.

This star Sirius is the perfect celestial description and representation of the cosmic union of both man and woman and God and man. I believe this is the celestial example of Jesus Christ and his disciples and the nation of Israel of old, and Adam and Eve before then.

Sirius with its companion emerging from its side: photographed with a 24-inch refracting telescope at Sroul Observatory.

This is a photograph of Sirius with its white dwarf, not as a red giant as the ancients saw it. One must envision Sirius B the white dwarf in this photo as a red giant with its companion Sirius the brightest star of the night sky coming out from its side when it appeared every fiftieth year marking for the feast of Jubilee. It is also in harmony with the years of Jesus' life when placing his birth date at 14B.C. also making Jesus of Nazareth the Jubilee Feast as you will see in the next chapter.

Seeing that Sirius is the brightest star in the sky and this fifty year cycle would have been seen by the ancients in the backdrop of the red giant, without any doubt, this does explain why so many of the ancient cultures possessed the knowledge and mechanics of this star system before modern man's discovery in 1862.

But what cannot be explained away by man is how the ancients knew and foretold of this star changing in color as the earth approached the precessional wobble, and of all the cultures of earth only one foretold of this coming change and only a remnant of that culture can grasp its meaning today, for as Sirius is the heavenly station of Adam and Eve. The nation of ancient Israel, the daughters of Zion, the daughters of Jerusalem, the bride of the Lord of Hosts, the bride of the Lamb, the New Jerusalem to come; in all of these analogies she is prophesied as though her sins are as scarlet (ruddy red). She shall be purified and made whiter than snow. These are they who have washed their robes and are made them white in the blood (for the life is in the blood) of the Lamb.

Again, what was made into mythologies of the past, with the other ancient cultures of the world with Isis of Egypt, Ishtar of Babylon, Dianna of Greece, and all the multitudes of goddesses, adorned as the Queen of Heaven by these cultures: None of them possessed the foreknowledge or foretold of the event that this star, which was the representation of the heavenly counterpart of their Goddesses, would undergo this metamorphosis and change from a red giant star to a small brilliant white star.

This foreknowledge has been reserved for the priesthood after the order of Melchizedek alone. The Levitical priesthood did not know, only the prophets: Yet even as many as have accepted the mind of the living Christ and acknowledge the actions of the life of Jesus of Nazareth as the plumb line of righteousness even to this very day they know, what I share here is true.

> The Heavens declare the glory of God: and the firmament show His handiwork. Day after day it utters his speech and night after night shows his knowledge. There is no speech nor language where

their voice is not heard. Their good news has gone out through all the earth and their words to the end of the world. He has set his tabernacle in the sun among them. He is as a bridegroom coming out of his chamber, and rejoices as a strong man to run a race His going forth is from the end of the heaven and his circuit unto the ends thereof there is nothing hid from the mist of his breath. Psalm 19:1-6

As the time draws nearer and nearer what seems to be an eternity to man is but a short space in time to the Father. All these things are happening in their proper time. Sirius dazzling brilliantly white is the sign of the coming of the son of man, and that his bride is being made ready.

The other ancient cultures of the world saw their religions and mythology as divine perfection just as they were. Even so with the Levitical priesthood. As then even now. As with all the religions of the world today.

Only the priesthood after the Order of Melchizedek saw then and sees now the ongoing preparation of the bride by the cleansing of the human condition by the Living Word of the Most High God; so that even the very composition and existence of the stars in heaven are subject to Him that has set them in motion for the calling of the great gathering Amen.

CHAPTER 4

The King of Kings

What was the star that the Magi followed in the Gospel of Matthew? Some versions of the Bible call these Magi, Astrologers other versions wise man. Let us take this at face value and put as many things as we can in their proper perspective. These Magi visited Jerusalem and had an audience with King Herod. King Herod died in 4 B.C. So any time after this date is ruled out as the date of Jesus of Nazareth's birth. How much earlier can we look? In the Gospel of Luke it states that Caesar Augustus decreed a census.

There were two census done before the death of Herod the Great in 4 B.C. these were done in 27 B.C. and 12 B.C. I believe 14 B.C. is the actual date of the birth of Jesus. In 12 B.C. Cyrenius first began his administrative rule in Syria, this date is also the same year that Herod exterminated the last of the male hiers of the Hyrcanus family which could have laid claim to the throne of Judea. According to the gospel of Matthew all males of two years of age and under were executed. This order came from the infomation that Herod gleaned from the Magi.

At around this time Herod's paranoia was so infamous that he even began killing his own sons. Augustus Caesar would later say of Herod: "Safer to be Herod's hog than to be one of his sons". This is the only explanation that harmonizes the Gospels of Matthew and Luke, concerning the date of Jesus' birth with the historical and political dyamics of the time.

Let us entertain this earlier date of 14 B.C. This would put Jesus at age forty-seven at the time of His crucifixion. In the Gospel of John, Jesus tells the scribes and Pharisees "Abraham rejoiced to see my day and he saw it and he was glad." Then the scribes and Pharisees said to him you're not yet fifty years old and you say you have seen Abraham. Notice they didn't say you're just barely thirty years old, or they didn't even say you're not even forty years old! But they did say you're not yet fifty years old. Let us assume that these people talking to Jesus, these scribes and Pharisees, had done some research on this guy. They had accused him of being a bastard son, and they saw him as bucking their positions of authority. It only figures they also knew his age to insinuate such an accusation of his birth. With this in mind 14 B.C. is not only plausible it is logical.

On January 6th 14 B.C. the constellation Leo rose directly over Judea if viewed from the Sphinx in Egypt just after sunset. The star Regulas is the heart star of the constellation of Leo, it is also the king of the stars according to Astrologers and Astronomers alike. The constellation of Leo is also known as "The Lion of Judah" to both as well. At this same time, it was in conjunction with Jupiter, and Jupiter is known as King of the planets together in this conjunction, they are the conjunction of the King of Kings.

The King of Kings

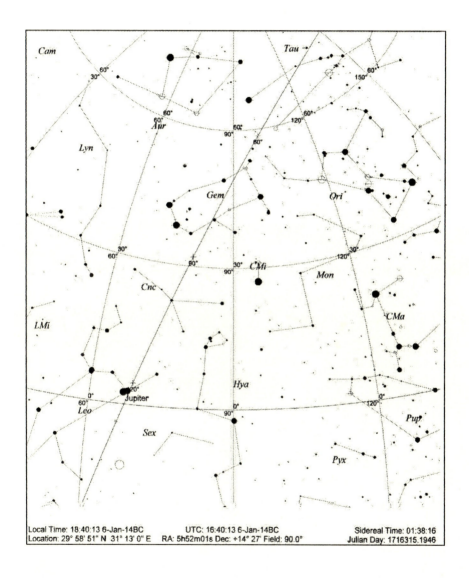

Regulas in its farthest movement north in its precessional course reaches an azimuth of 28 degrees due north of this Astro-marker the Sphinx in Egypt. This is very significant as it declares who this King of Kings is by actually pointing to his place of birth.

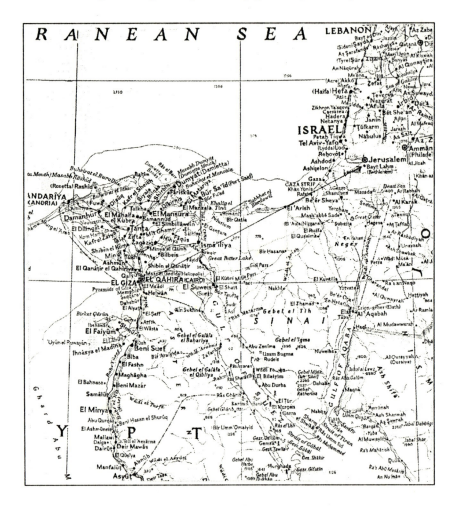

The King of Kings

If we look at this conjunction from the ancient home land of the Magi of the east, from their location at Persepolis in ancient Persia: This King of Kings conjunction is descending to earth directly over Bethlehem in Judea, in the western sky in the early morning as the sun is about to rise in the east. This happens on the same night as it rose earlier that evening over Bethlehem when viewed from Egypt.

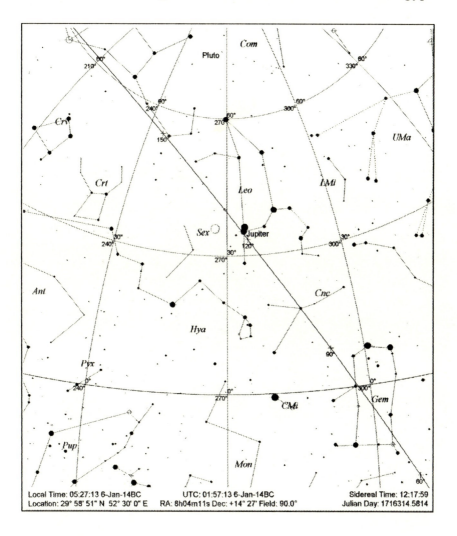

The Way of Melchizedek

This geographic map also points to the place where this universal King of Kings was expected be born, as it was viewed from the Magi's home land at the ancient city of Persepolis.

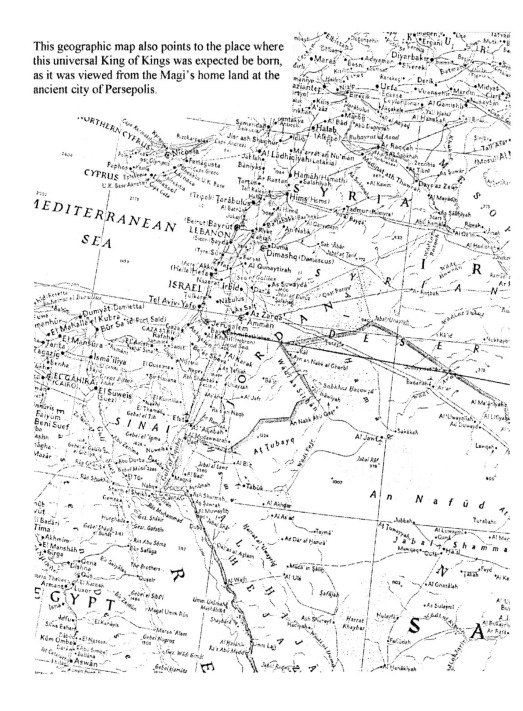

The King of Kings

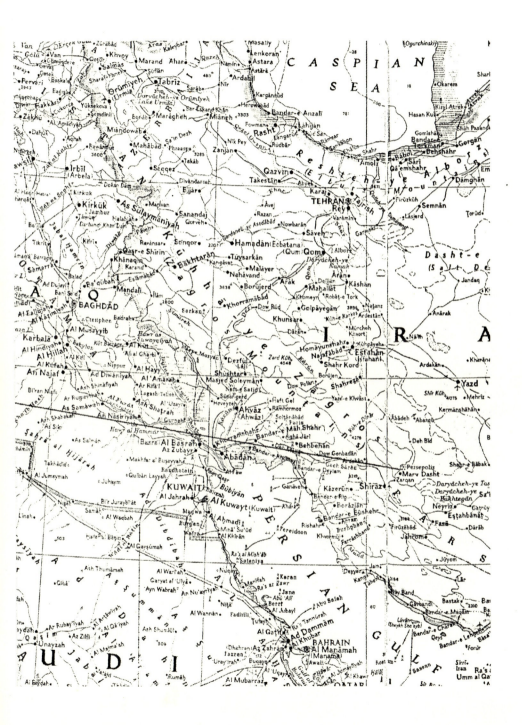

In the ancient Egyptian mythology Osiris (Orion) is not fully risen until Isis (Sirius) is risen and Isis (Sirius) is not fully risen until Horus is born. Horus is not considered born until Regulas is in its helical rising.

We now will consider the constellation of Leo. How does it enter into the picture with Orion and the star Sirius? What is significant with Leo is the exact timing of its helical rising after the helical rising of Orion and its location of its rising on the horizon from the Sphinx. Again we need to remind ourselves of what Jesus said to Mary Magdalene, the woman that anointed the feet of Jesus with spices and tears then dried them with her hair, and then later visited his tomb the morning of his resurrection.

When she saw Jesus outside of his tomb on that morning, the morning of the third day after the Passover, as Mary came to recognize Jesus, she moved to embrace him, but Jesus told her:

> "Touch me not for I have not yet ascended to My Father." But go to my brethren and say to them. I ascend to my Father and your Father to my God and your God. John 20: 17

In all four of the Gospels Jesus tells his disciples when he goes to the father he will send the Holy Ghost, and they would be baptized in the Holy Ghost and in fire with power and in truth. When this had taken place Jesus of Nazareth was no longer just the Lamb of God, the Passover. He is now both the Passover Lamb and the Lion of the tribe of Judah having overcome death.

As it is fifty days from Passover to Pentecost, it is also forty seven days from his resurrection to Pentecost and the coming of the Holy Ghost. It is also fifty days from the moment of the first stars' appearance in Orion's belt until the helical rising of Regulas, the heart star of the constellation of Leo. It is also forty seven days from the time Al Nitak, the brightest and last star of Orion's belt clears the horizon, until the helical rising of Regulas also.

This is illustrated with star charts from the "Sky Map" astronomy program on the next two pages. Both charts show the elapsed time of the helical rising of Regulas in correlation to the helical rising of Orion.

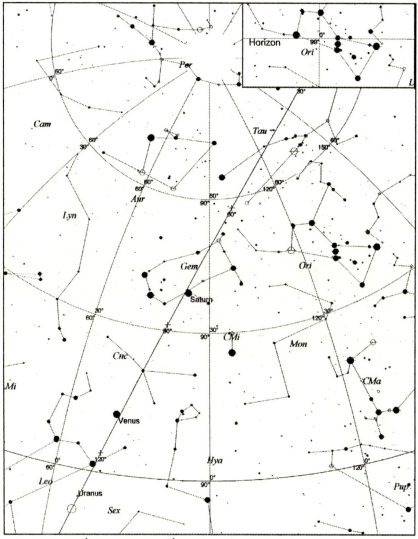

The 50th day after 18th of June 33 A.D. time 04:46 AM

The Way of Melchizedek

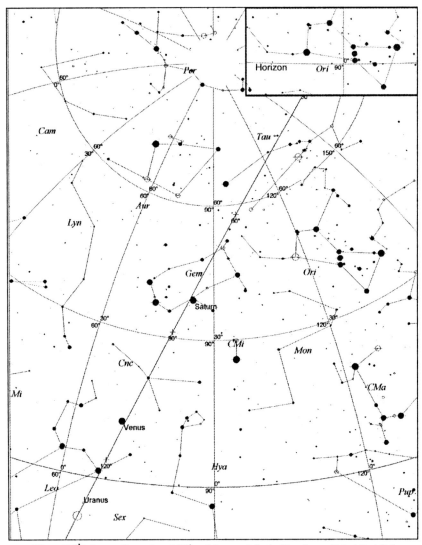

The 47ᵗʰ day after the 21ˢᵗ of June 33 A.D. time 04:46 AM

The King of Kings

This rising also corresponds perfectly with the event of Jesus Christ's resurrection, three days in rising and forty seven days later he sending the Holy Ghost on Pentecost. At this moment his disciples and his bride are fully risen with Him.

Though the event of Jesus' crucifixion, resurrection, and his ascension to the right hand of the Father, and the coming of the Holy Ghost at Pentecost do not take place on the same day as the astronomical events took place in the sky just before sunrise. They do show the timing of both are exact in that the stars are displaying the events of Jesus of Nazareth chronologically as they happened on earth in the year circa 33 A.D. and 14 B.C.

It is in bringing these events of the Great cycle of 25,920 years into focus with our solar cycle of 365 days, one year, the inner wheel, that together we can see the mechanical processes of the cosmic clock of our universe, and the purpose of God for mankind.

This wheel the solar cycle is the inner wheel in the middle of a greater wheel, the stellar cycle. It is reminiscent of the vision of the prophet Ezekiel. Ezekiel's wheels are made of living creatures in kind as the Zodiac is also made of creatures. Interestingly similar to Jacob's prophecies of his sons from pages 21 and 22.

The synchronizing factor in the calibration and observation of both the Great wheel and the inner wheel in respect to biblical prophecy is they are both perfectly in tune with the Astro-marker of the Great Sphinx.

Most of the technical data thus far has been from this location. The following pages will illustrate this phenomenon in perfect detail. The conclusion that I have arrived at is that the Sphinx design and purpose was and is to acknowledge the promised redeemer that transcends all the cultures. While we of earth have grave markers, he has a birth marker. With the mounting evidence I accept the notion that the Sphinx and Egyptian Mythology are derivatives of an earlier culture.

This crouching figure of a lion with the face of a man at Giza in Egypt, the Sphinx, is the centerpiece of an astronomical observatory of such complexity, and done with such precision, that its precise measurements and Astro-calculations could not be duplicated until the latter part of the twentieth century. This observatory is also the center of much debate, in the academic community, concerning the date of its construction. The consensus of most Egyptologists place the time of the Sphinx construction at about 2500 B.C. While most geologists and paleoclimatologists agree with a growing minority of Egyptologists that the Sphinx has a minimum age of 6,000 years. Approximately 4000 B.C. and these are considered conservative estimates.

But the precision of its design and its alignment and location with the summer and winter solstices are undeniable.

The sun rises 28 degrees to the north of due east of the Sphinx on the summer solstice. Conversely, it rises 28 degree to the south on the winter solstice.

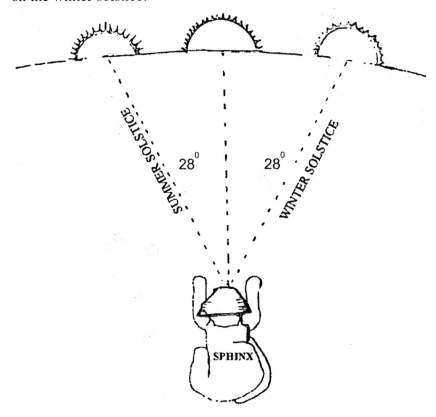

Sunrise of the four seasons of the year from the view of the Sphinx at Giza

The Sphinx association with Egyptian mythology is as complex as it is precise as an astronomical marker. It was associated with the Egyptian god of creation, the father of the gods, Atum, later also known as Amen. It was used as part of an elaborate ceremony commemorating the past deeds of the Egyptian deity Horus, also in association with the Pharaohs of Egypt in their journey to the afterlife as the reincarnation of Horus. In a faithful reenactment of Horus in his quest to his father Osiris.

In addition to these aspects, the Sphinx's counterpart in the heavens is the constellation of Leo. The constellation of Leo is representative of both Horus the God king, unifier of the two realms, in his quest to his father, just as the constellation of Leo follows after the constellation of Orion through the night sky.

And upon completing his task Horus is coalesced with Atum becoming a composite deity, the fulfiller of the task becoming one with the Father God becoming the Amen-Ra.

Also the constellation of Leo was the constellation representing kingship in general throughout the world of ancient astrology, even as with the zodiac of today Leo is the symbol of kingship or leadership. So also is Leo's earthly counterpart, the crouching lion of the Great Sphinx, so is Leo. The two are meant to be seen as one and the same.

Let us now return to the subject of Jacob. Did he see his sons as the Zodiac, as the essence of the mechanical wheel of heaven itself?

Judah is the son of Jacob and Jacob speaks in the following prophecy:

> Judah you are he whom your brothers shall praise: Your hand shall be at the neck of your enemies. Your fathers shall bow down before you. Judah is a lion's whelp; from the prey, my son, you are gone up; he stooped down, he crouched as a lion, and as a young lion; who shall rouse him up? The scepter shall not depart from Judah, nor a lawgiver from between his feet, until Shi-loh come. Unto him shall the gathering be. Binding his foal unto the vine, and his ass's colt. Unto the choice vine He washes his garment in

wine, and his cloths in the blood of grapes. His eyes shall be red with wine, and his teeth white with milk. Genesis 49:8-12

It is verse nine and ten that I find compelling. In these two verses Jacob not only describes his son with all the same symbolism and mannerisms and traits as the constellation of Leo, he is describing the astronomical alignments of the Great Sphinx to the tee, as the personification of his son Judah's future lineage. Jacob surely saw the Great Sphinx and he knew with prior knowledge that it gazed into the future foretelling the coming of the Messiah and the place of his birth. Having been in Egypt himself at the time he spoke this of the son Judah.

The Egyptian priesthood saw this astro-marker, the Sphinx, as the keystone memorial in order to honor their Pharaohs in their journey to the afterlife by the commemoration of the mythology of the religion of state, thus commemorating their past.

But the priesthood of Melchizedek is a knowledge of prophesy of what the Most High is going to do in the future. Being of this order of Melchizedek, Jacob knew in the spirit in which he prophesied concerning his son Judah, the providence of God would take hold in world events.

Now applying the knowledge that the Sphinx could possibly predate the fourth dynasty, the dynasty which the majority of Egyptologists believe is responsible for the construction of the Sphinx, by nearly 2,000 years, there is the possibility an advanced pre-Egyptian culture was the architect and builders. But yet undeniably, the Great Sphinx is an astronomical marker. Let's continue on the course of 28 degrees due north and due south beyond the horizon and the rising points of the summer and winter solstices on the plateau of Giza to see if there are any significant landmarks of importance.

Traveling 28 degrees south from the Sphinx within its paws on its winter solstice course for approximately one hundred and eighty miles you come to Mt Horeb, ie. Mt Sinai. Where Moses receives the Law and gives it to the nation of Israel! Traveling 28 degrees north on the course of the summer solstice for approximately three hundred and sixty km you arrive at Bethlehem of Judea, the birthplace of Jesus Christ!

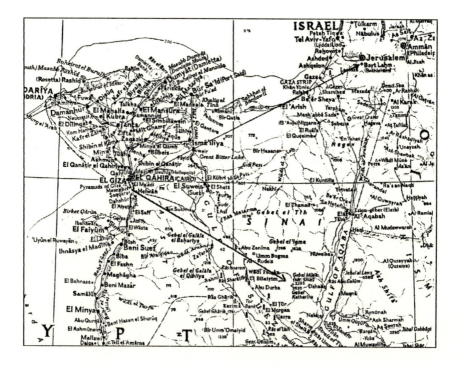

What exactly is the Sphinx? The Sphinx is the symbol of God in his people in the Congregation of mankind, waiting for the Gathering to take place.

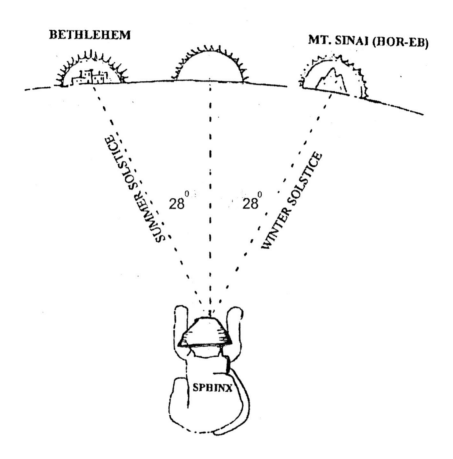

These alignments are exact; they are perfect in both directions north and south, without exception.

If the Great Sphinx had been built five miles east or west of its present location, it still would function as an observatory for what the Egyptians were using it for. Only in its exact longitude and latitude where it now sits, is it capable to meeting the criteria spoken by Jacob to be simultaneously an astronomical marker for the two solstices with Mt. Horeb and Bethlehem being within the disc of the sun at its rising.

So we have the lawgiver Moses, and Jesus Christ, the King of Kings the scepter holder between the feet of this lion. This is a testimony in itself to whom the architects of the Great Sphinx are. This also illustrates the prophecy spoken by Jacob. "The scepter shall not depart from Judah nor a Lawgiver from between his feet." Gen 49:10.

The prominent Egyptologist Mark Lehner has looked for a legendary secret passage under the forepaws of the Sphinx for more than thirty years without success. The Hall of Records that he has so long searched for has two books. One is the Lamb's Book of Life and the other is the Book of Deeds. Rev 20:11-15

Mark, Jesus is that secret passage, and the Hall of Records, is the judgment that every soul that has ever lived shall find themselves standing before as the books are opened this is the passage you have looked for, death to life or death to death or life to death or life to life.

CHAPTER 5

The Southern Cross

O ur next investigation focuses on the constellation of the Southern Cross. At the time that Abraham received the promise that the Messiah of mankind would be born from his descendents and this One would redeem (Buy Back) mankind, the Southern Cross was much higher above the horizon than it is today. At the time of Abraham this constellation reached the height of 8 degrees in the night sky above the southern horizon at an azimuth of 28 degrees west of due south from Abraham's home in Hebron in Cannan at 10:15 May 1st 1871 B.C.

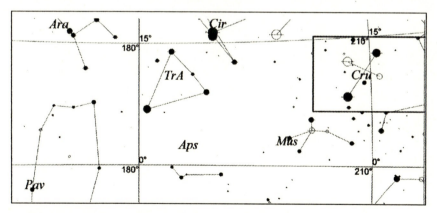

Southern Cross From Hebron at 10:15 May 1st 1871 B.C.

At this time the Lord told Abraham in a dream that his seed would be four hundred years a sojourner in a strange land to the fourth generation. Gen: 15: 1-17

If one looks at this from the perspective in which it is written, and the duality of the nature of the scriptures as they are written this brings to light a deeper meaning to this event. From the time of the rise of the Thebian Kings of Egypt which replaced the Hyksos Kings who were either Semitic or under the Semitic influence of Joseph who also describes his own person as "Apotheosis" to become like God. Gen 50:19

According to Egyptologists the last Pharaoh of the Hyksos was named Apophis and the meaning of his name was the same as the attribute described by Joseph. His center of power was based in Memphis at the time of its collapse in the year 1567 B.C. From this date of 1567 B.C. moving forward in time by four, four hundred year generations we arrive at the year 33 A.D. At midnight of that day when Jesus of Nazareth is executed the Southern Cross touched the horizon 19 degrees west of due south of Jerusalem, if one takes into account for the slightly higher elevation southwest of Jerusalem. Now by drawing an azimuth from the Temple Mount it will line up with first Mt Zion then Bethlehem and finally with Mt Sinai. This exclaims astronomically both the method and the price paid for this redemption and who was destined to pay for the penalty of sin for us all that was enforced by the Law of Moses inaugurated at Mt Sinai.

The Southern Cross

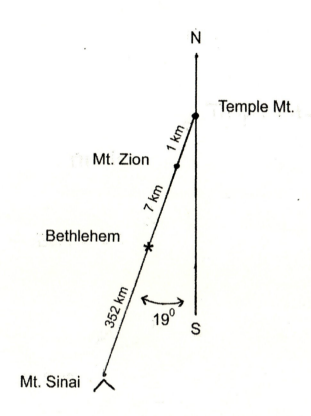

19 degree azimuth from Jerusalem to Mt Sinai

The Way of Melchizedek

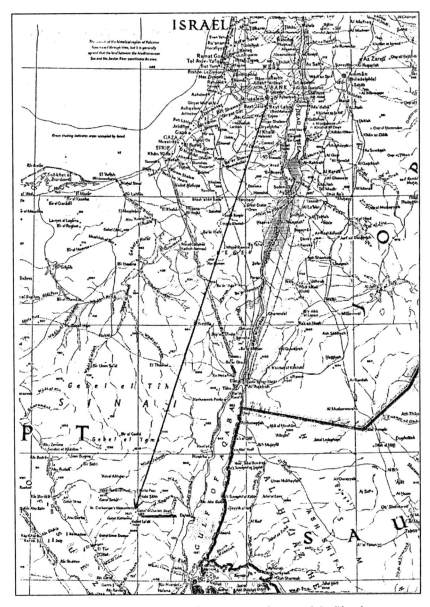

19 degree Azimuth from Jerusalem to Mt Sinai

The Southern Cross

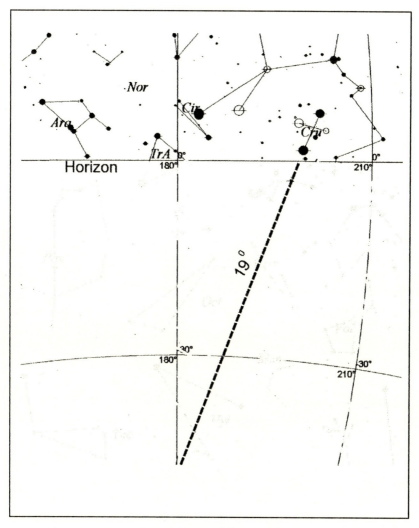

Jerusalem to Mt. Sinai

Astronomical Map 19 degrees west of due south
May 1st 33 A.D. at 10:15

The Southern Cross rose over the horizon earlier that evening and set later that night duplicating the degrees of the sunrise of the summer and winter solstice from the Sphinx in Egypt.

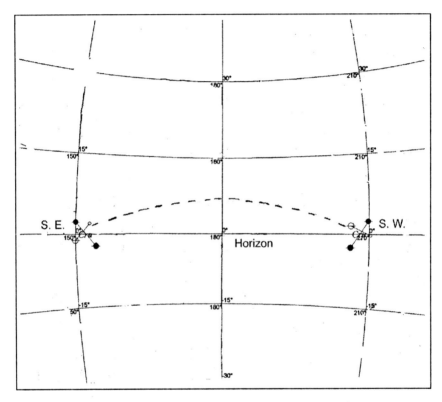

The Southern Cross rising at 5:11 PM on May 1st 33 A.D.
The Southern Cross setting at 11:05 AM on May 1st 33 A.D.

It is completely impossible for all these astronomical alignments to be synchronized with the timing and description of the events that took place at this time in history, and to coincide with the characterization of these ancient prophecies by coincidents. The next question is could ancient man of his own accord have been capable of correctly making all these calculations and seeing to the engineering of this singular event in time. How could they have known that Sirius the ancient red giant was to change into a white dwarf within the next few generations after the crucifixion of Jesus of Nazareth? To the skeptic all I can say is I am only relating the historical astronomical events that have taken place in the past and reminding the reader what is written in prophecy that said all these things were foretold to come to pass. Any scientist even if he or she is completely without faith that is a scientist indeed, whether Astronomer, Archeologist or Anthropologist or Egyptologist must concede these are the facts that are presented here, or disqualify him or herself as a scientist completely, and relegate themselves to the cult of secular Humanism.

Now returning to the constellation of the Southern Cross the highest star at the top of this constellation will disappear below the horizon from the highest vantage point in Jerusalem which is Mt Golgotha symbolically signifying the closing of the window of the dispensation of the work of forgiveness manifest by Jesus of Nazareth at his crucifixion. This takes place at the same approximate time as the wobble of the Earth's axis that was prophesied by Isaiah, Daniel and John concerning the judgment of the nations and the wrath of God on the wicked and the deliverance of the saints the followers of the Most High God.

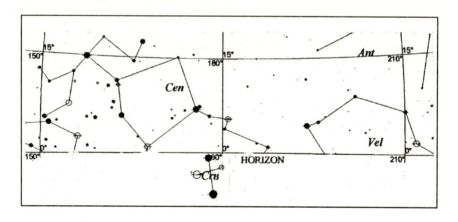

The Southern Cross at 9:39 P.M. May 1st 2453 A.D.

CHAPTER 6

The Gulf of the Serpent

There is one more constellation to be examined in this unfolding mystery of mankind's history. This constellation is Hydra the serpent, and what it represents. What caused this divergence in the approach of the Most High? The question that is most important to all concerned is simple. Why is there such a gulf between these camps in their approach to divinity? The answer is so simple it is frightening and that answer exists in the presences of naked reality. It is to be chosen; the elect, for them it is the gift of faith; with patience, the very verb of being; being in the presence, and in the presence at rest, a gift. On the other hand there are those in the very sense of the verb are hiding yet trying and seeking to keep a connection with the very one that they hide from. From this comes all religion.

These are the determining factors in ones' approach to the Most High, coupled with ambition and vanity in the form of pride, especially national pride, which is the determining factor of this schism.

There are a few definitive examples we can examine. The Magi ie. Magician and wizards of the various cultures of ancient times operated much as they do today. Whether by incantations, spells or potions, simply put, they used formulas whether spiritual or chemical, or Astrological, simply formulas in an attempt to operate the mechanics of heaven. This is "magic" whether by any of the name or philosophy or mythology, not excluding many of them that call themselves Christians, they also make attempts of magic by invoking the name Jesus at the end of their partitions as though sounding the syllables of his name alone will work magic for them.

Here are some definitive examples between the priesthood of Melchizedek the election, and they that practice magic under whatever name.

This very difference in the application of the kingdom of heaven is clearly exemplified in Deuteronomy 11:10-14: as a shadow of things to come.

> For the land you are about to go into to possess is not as the land of Egypt from where you came. Where you sewed your seed and watered your seed with the labor of your feet, to bring water to your gardens and your herbs. But the land which I bring you to possess is a land of hills and valleys. That drink is the water of the rain of heaven. It is a land which YAHWEH your God provides for. The eyes of YAHWEH are always upon it, from the beginning of the year even to the end of the year. It shall come to pass if you will harken diligently to my commandments that I command you this day and give to you this day, to love YAHWEH your God and to serve him with all your hearts and all your soul. I will give you the rain of your land in His due season. The first rain and the latter rain that you may gather in the corn and your wine and oil.

I am here to say these passages are not just talking about farming in the natural land. Rather, they are speaking of the approach of the applications of the powers of the kingdom of heaven. If then a kingdom, all in it is the possession of its King.

On the one hand the wizards and magicians working their formulas to obtain their increase; speaking in spiritual terms, displaying ambition for power presumptively and self willfulness. On the other hand the prophets and priests after the order of

Melchizedek of the Most High. These receive their increase by believing the promise of God, that He will give his rain, his **revelation** in his own time these are they that rest in his promise and move at his direction. The one is motivated by gain, ambition and the lust of power and knowledge as a means of gaining preeminence. The other is motivated in the peace of being at rest by faith; and go only when they are sent by the King of Heaven. The order of Magic takes to possess. The order of the Most High gives as it is given to them.

Jesus describes this principle in his teachings and his life itself. In one such teaching he said: "The kingdom of heaven suffers violence and the violent take it by force." Then in the Gospel of John 10:1-3 he speaks saying:

> Truly truly I say to you, he who does not enter by the door into the sheepfold but climbs up some other way, the same is a thief and robber. But he that enters in by the door is the shepherd of the flock. To him the doorkeeper opens the door, and the flock hear his voice and he calls his own by their names and brings them forth

St. John 10:9-10 Goes on

> I am the door; if any one enters by me he shall be saved, and shall go in and out and find good pastures. The thief does not come, except to steal and kill and to destroy; But I have come that they might have life, and have it abundantly.

As with the earlier scripture in Deuteronomy, this speaks of the spiritual pastures. Taking these scriptures into consideration, I am here to tell you, those that use some kind of formula to obtain power, their intent will be made manifest by their actions. Whatsoever form of magic it may be, they will be made to account for what they have taken. Those that enter by the verb that is in the "resting" in the being of Jesus he will allow them to pass and will give freely to them. Those whose intent is not in his rest even they are practicing magic. Even when they tack Jesus' own name on to their partitions yet their own hearts are not right with him for what they seek they seek to possess. They have been deceived.

As for the magician and the wizard, and those who invoke incantations and spells with the help of some kind of "helper" spirit, they obtain what it is they seek by theft. They have not passed through his rest, they have gone about another way and not by the door. They have trespassed and taken what is not theirs. They know in their hearts there is a price to pay for the virtue they have stolen. Yet, in their folly they claim God is a force in the universe that can be used for good or for evil depending on the motive of the practitioner, but yet they offer a price for what they have gained.

Does one have intellectual dialogue with a universal force? Does a universal force make promises to individuals? Would a universal force take payment for what had been obtained on behalf of the practitioner? Therefore, deep in their own hearts they know they lie, even to themselves. In that they offer a ransom to appease and satisfy those counterfeit spirits that obtained what it was they ask for. They are defrauded of the ransom they have paid, and the trespassing will be laid at their feet. For the agents to whom they made payment were not the servants of the Doorkeeper, they are but thieves.

I speak now to those who use the name of Jesus as though it is magic, even as we all have, in our ignorance, in the past. Forgive us of our trespasses as we forgive those who trespass against us.

The Doorkeeper provides for all freely who pass through him without cost to those who enter into his rest. They that offer payment to those who enter another way do so because they themselves cannot look the Doorkeeper in the eye. For he sees the intents and motives of the heart. So they hire the thief. If they continue in their ways and do not change in their hearts, to see the Doorkeeper eye to eye, in peace, their reward will be with the thieves whom they have employed. This is the price for the lust of preeminence, it will be paid with the soul.

As also the ancients of past times were unwilling to accept the purpose of God by reason of their pride, they also were unwilling to acknowledge the Chosen Universal King of Kings and refashioned the truth into a lie and in doing so alienated themselves from the Living God by their nationalistic conceit. The knowledge they had received in times past they were now in rebellion to. They refashioned what they did know of God's heaven to glorify themselves and sought connection with God by looking back to what their imaginations called the origin of creation. The beginning of man with God: to legitimize their places with the Creator believing through elaborate rituals and commemorations of the first time, that they called the Zep Tepi. By this the magicians of Egypt hoped that this would reconnect them with God. In their vanity they placed their ancestors in the place of God's chosen "One." With magic they tried in vain to recreate his rest.

The liturgy of the Egyptian book of the dead is the mythology of the pantheon of the Egyptian deities. It is the commemoration of the deeds of Osiris, Isis and Horus and the belief their Pharaohs were the reincarnation of these deities. Believing that this would unify them with the Gods, these people would faithfully follow the rituals prescribed by their priests. Each Pharaoh would reenact the deeds of Osiris and Horus so they also could return to the Zep Tepi and live again with their fathers, the Gods. Great pomp and preparation were carefully followed that all things were observed. This was done by every Pharaoh. They would take all their earthly treasures with them on their great journey to their father's as their father before them had, over and over for millennia after millennia.

What of their great treasures they took with them? Stolen by grave robbers. What of their bodies? Exhumed and made a spectacle of in museums, if they were lucky. But most became firewood for Bedouin campfires. The road to Rostau is a dead end. This is what Jesus was communicating, when one of his disciples first wanted to send off his father before following Jesus. He said, "Follow me: and let the dead bury their dead." Isaiah wrote:

> The princes of Zoan have become fools, the priests of Memphis have become haughty and deceive Egypt. Even the foundation of all her families (Pharaoh). Isaiah

The Way of Melchizedek

The Princes of Zoan and Priesthood of Memphis mentioned by Isaiah are the definitive examples of nationalistic pride. These multitudes of variations and philosophies of God, and the after-life, intermingled with nationalism encompassed nearly the entire ancient world. It is this commemoration of tradition which these many different people believed was the foundation for connection with God or their Gods in the Egyptians case. Believing by faithfully performing their rituals and devotions as the means of linking themselves with the Creator, and returning to the genesis of time with their Gods or God, they believed they found justification. This is the blueprint of all religions except one. This form of religion is the very antithesis of the Order of Melchizedek. No matter how well it was or is packaged and presented.

In an obscure dissertation by the prophet Ezekiel and the prophet Isaiah, they describe the mind of the serpent who has devised all these religions:

> How is it that you have fallen from heaven, O Lucifer, son of the Mourning! How is it that you are cut down to the ground, you who weaken the nations of the earth. For you have said in your heart I will ascend into heaven. I will exalt my throne above the children of God: I will sit also upon the mount of the congregation in the sides of the north. I will ascend above the heights of the clouds: I will be like the Most High: Isaiah 14:12-14.

Look at this statement: <u>I will exalt my throne above the children of God</u>. Let the intent of this statement become crystal clear. His intent is rule over and dictate to the congregation.

Look at the next statement: <u>I will sit upon the mount of the congregation in the sides of the north.</u> Let his intent be clear. The mount of the congregation is 28 degrees to the north side of the congregation, this is the place of the King of Kings. His intent is to take the place of the King of Kings, to be the Vicar of the King of Kings. The word vicar in the dictionary means to take the place of; and this is just not in title only: It is in deed as well, any who put themselves above the children of God put themselves in the place of the King of Kings they are they that want to rule over the congregation.

Look at this next statement: <u>I will ascend above the heights of the clouds</u>: His intent is his dictation is to have precedence over the Prophet's past, present, and future making his word the law; and the tradition to be followed.

As Jesus' disciples began to argue over who would lead after his departure Jesus made clear to them saying:

> The kings of the Gentiles exercise lordship over them: and they that exercise authority upon them are called benefactors. But you shall not do so: but he that is greatest among you, let him be as the younger; and he that is chief, as he that serves.

This statement by Jesus shows the same consciousness as the prophet Isaiah for all to understand what is not to be the way. Now Ezekiel's testimony is:

> This says the Lord GOD: In you was sealed up the sum, full of wisdom and perfect beauty. You have been in Eden, the garden of God. Every precious stone was your covering, the ruby, topaz and the diamond, the beryl, the onyx and the jasper, the sapphire, the emerald and the carbuncle and gold: The workmanship of your tabrets and of your pipes was prepared in you the day that you were created. You are the anointed cherub that covereth and I have made you so. You were upon the holy mountain of God: You have walked up and down through the midst of the Urim and Thumbim the stones of fire. You were perfect in your ways from the day that you were created, until iniquity was found in you. By the multitude of your prosperity; This has filled your inward parts with vanity that you are violent. I will cast you out from the holy mountain of God as

> profane. I will destroy you O covering Cherub, from the midst of the stones of fire. Your heart was lifted up because of your beauty. You have corrupted your wisdom by reason of your brightness. I will cast you to the ground and the kings of the earth will behold you made low. You have defiled your sanctuaries by the multitude of your vanities by the vanity of your traffic Therefore will I bring forth a fire inside your own self and it shall devour you, and I will bring you to ashes upon the earth in the sight of all them that look to you. All they that know you among the people shall be astonished at you. And you shall be a terror to them no more.

It is when this covering Cherub discovered that his station and authority was only temporal is what brought forth his vanity and violence and he knew his lot was cast with Satan. He learned his fate from the Prophets after the order of Melchizedek. As Adam and Eve were in the garden of God; so Judah was also the garden of God an Eden the hedged garden of the vine of God from which the Branch has now come Amen. At this moment the awareness of this covering cherub with all his given glory discovered he was nothing but an allegory and proverb of Satan. It is this being, this serpent the beguiler of Adam and Eve, that deceived Adam and Eve to eat the fruit of the tree of knowledge of good and evil that was forbidden for them to eat, and why was it forbidden? For in eating of it they set for themselves thrones of judgment in heaven and decided what was good and evil for themselves on their own. In doing so, they judged God's creation with their own eyes. So, they came to be as God passing judgment over creation, just as the serpent told them. What God saw as good they saw as evil.

Every day they had met with God, before they had taken of the tree of the knowledge of good and evil, and they were naked. To God, this was fine, it was good they were hiding nothing. After taking of the tree they knew they were naked and hid themselves for they saw their own nakedness as evil. They had become judges in opposition with their creator thus they made themselves adversaries with their Father, God.

To keep the separation from being permanent, the Lord put them out of his garden and barred the way to the tree of Life. So, man was on earth and God in heaven. Yet the tree of the knowledge of good and evil was not evil in itself. It was the result of taking from the tree that separated man from God. The Lord told them that one would come to undo what had been done.

So God took his knowledge of good and evil as he saw good and evil and planted this tree on earth by the hand of a man named Moses. Then, God told Moses to tell the people that had multiplied on the earth, "He that keeps every writ of the law will live forever, he that breaks its least infraction will surely die the death." This God did knowing no man of earth could do this and he alone could keep his Law. This is the beginning of the completion of the promise made to Adam and Eve, and to Noah and his sons, to Abraham, Isaac, and to Jacob this was the redeemer that would come and keep all the law prescribed by Moses this they all waited for. For as Abraham offered his most precious, God sent his, and all the law was kept. Being spotless he kept all the Law, he ate of God's tree of good and evil and kept all God's precepts and all his statutes so that he and he alone can live forever. This is the Lord Jesus Christ. In his life has all the Law been kept and he has made the payment for redemption of man with his own life, and his Father looked upon his soul and was satisfied and said; "it is done." This is the promise of the Father and the Son that all that look to Jesus' life as the fulfillment of God the Father's Law will live in him.

Those that clothe themselves with his body that was crucified, God will put his son's words in that person's heart and he will be satisfied that that person has acknowledged his Law. As the Law is good and all men will be judged by the Law. Those that accept the mind of the living Christ as the fulfiller of the Law will live in him and his spirit will begin its work in that person's heart for all the rest of that persons life as many as believe that God has risen Jesus from the dead.

This is God's testimony and Promise of the Redeemer that no one can keep the Law but God, and only God can eat of that tree and live. By this Law Jesus took up his life again in the body of a man and lives forevermore. It is by this he has set in motion that all men will be forgiven even as they forgive others. This is the everlasting covenant between God and man, Christ in you.

Moses is the embodiment of Lucifer before Lucifer fell from his place in heaven, when he was yet perfect in his ways. Even as the Prophet Ezekiel spoke. By the time of King David and the Prophets the Levitical priesthood had come to be the embodiment of the accuser Lucifer after his fall from heaven. When in his vanity with violence both he and they sought to be above the stars of heaven, which is to say above the children of God. This was the message spoken to the Levitical priesthood by the Prophets of the Order after the way of Melchizedek concerning the coming of the Messiah, and the Levitical priesthood opposed it. They killed the Prophets that spoke this message and killed the Messiah when he came.

When Jesus was in the Temple at Jerusalem the High Priests came upon him while he was teaching the people and questioned him "By who's authority do you do these things and who gave you this authority?" Jesus answered "I will ask you a question and if you answer me, I will tell you by what authority I do these things. Where does the baptism of John come from? Is it from heaven or is it from men?" The High Priests said "we do not know so we can not answer you." So Jesus likewise did not answer them. But he did tell them in parables:

> There was a man who owned a house and planted a vineyard there. He fenced it and dug in it a winepress and built a tower, and then he leased it to laborers and went on a journey. When the fruit was at hand he sent his servants to the laborers, so he could receive the fruits of his vineyard. But the laborers seized his servants and beat some of them and stoned and killed others as well. Again he sent other servants more than the first time and they did the same thing to them as well. At last he sent his son to them saying they will honor my son. But when the laborers saw it was his son, they said to themselves: This is his heir; come, let us kill him and retain his inheritance. So

The Gulf of the Serpent

> they seized him, and took him outside the vineyard and they killed him. When the owner of the vineyard comes, what do you think he will do to those laborers? St Matthew 21:33-40

When he finished this parable he asked them what they thought about it, and their reply was;
"The owner of that vineyard will utterly destroy those miserable laborers, and put the vineyard in the hands of laborers that will give him the produce of his vineyard."
Jesus then said to them. "Have you not read in the scriptures?"

> The stone that the builders rejected the same is become the Chief Cornerstone. This is the Lords doing and it is marvelous In our eyes. Therefore I say to you the kingdom of God shall be taken from you and given to those people that bring forth its fruits. Whoever falls on this stone will be broken. But whomever this stone fall on will be ground into powder." When the chief priest heard this they sought to take him by force understanding he spoke this of them.

They in their vanity and violence did seek then and do seek even now to sit in the Redeemer's seat at the north side of the congregation. As do many others it is by their fruits you will know them. As the Egyptians persecuted the Hebrews, the Levitical Priesthood persecuted the order after Melchizedek. So it is with all those that are unwilling to submit their place to the Living God.

This is the representation of the constellation of Hydra the Serpent. If they whom are called to be the bride of the Most High look back over their shoulder have Lot's wife as a proverb; even as Sirius would need to look back over its shoulders to behold the constellation of Hydra.

The Prophet Isaiah's recorded witness is:

In this mountain shall the Lord of Hosts make unto all people a Feast of fat things, a feast of wines of circumspection, of fat things full of the marrow, of wines of circumspection well refined. And he will destroy in this mountain the face of the covering cast over all people and the veil that is spread over all nations. He will swallow up death in victory; and the Lord God will wipe away the tears from off all their faces; and the rebuke of his people shall he take away from off all the earth: for the Lord has spoken it. And it shall be said in that day, Lo this is our GOD. We have waited for him, and he will save us. This is the LORD. We have waited for him, we will be glad and rejoice in his salvation. Isaiah 25: 6-9

CHAPTER 7

The Way

The ministry of Jesus of Nazareth is expressed by two great issues, his message of the worship of the God of Abraham Isaac and Jacob, whom Jesus claimed as his father, before both the Jewish elite and commoner alike. He also directed his message at the results of their developing religious traditions.

This developing tradition that inter-mingled the Law of Moses with the traditions of the "learned elders" had evolved over generations; this is the stage which Jesus walked on to. In their own eyes these Jewish elite of their day were the most pious and zealous people conceivable. They micro-inspected every aspect of the Mosaic Law in accordance to their traditions, with more fervor and zeal than the past seventy two generations before them. For this kind of devotion they completely expected God's deliverance from the Romans. Yet instead of commending them, Jesus rebuked them, calling them the blind leading the blind, because they had neglected the most important part of the Law, the worship and reverence of the Voice of God as a living entity among them. Because of this lack of desire to draw close to the "Living God" is why he said this. They also lacked in understanding of the nature of God and his purpose, in more ways than just having compassion towards the less fortunate, and the oppressed, with kindness and hospitality of strangers. They focused on keeping a law that was a proverb of futility that none of them could keep. They as a people, choose not to enter into communion with God as Abraham Isaac and Jacob had done before them.

Moses had brought this people out of Egypt to Mount Horeb in Sinai, but instead of communing with God in the way their ancestors had, they insisted that Moses go up into the presence of God for them in their place. They feared the power and majesty and holiness they beheld from afar, and said to Moses: "What ever he tells you, we will do, but you go up for us on our behalf." For this lack of trust in a God that had shown such great mercy to them as he had, in delivering them from their oppression in Egypt, with signs and wonders. So they received what they had asked for, a law to keep instead of union with God, and a priesthood of fallible men that stood between them and God to make intersession on their behalf. But this could only mask their sins and was never able to remove them. They preferred this instead of communion with God as their fathers had. How was it they thought this God would now destroy or consume them if they communed with him, after all that he had done on their behalf? For this the Law they received became a burdensome proverb of futility. This was not the way of Abraham, Isaac or Jacob, this they had never done and such a burden they never had to bear.

Yet in all this, is the will of God seen in its due course, the Law they received and the feasts contained in it were given to them as a shadow of the "Promised One" to come. Who would keep all that was contained in the Law so that he would be the fulfillment and "completion" of the Law itself, even as God had promised Moses:

> I will raise them up a Prophet from among their brethren, like unto you, and I will put my words in his mouth; and he shall speak unto them all that I will command, it shall come to pass that whosoever will not hearken unto my words which he will speak in my name I will require it of that person. Moses Deut 18:15-19

So this was the Law they so zealously took pride in, with their

The Way

pompous praise they glorified themselves at how well they thought they kept this Law. But the Law they commemorated as a "thing" in the past was meant to be observed as what was to come in the future. They had not learned this, or why they had this law in the first place. Not even generation after generation, and prophet after prophet speaking the admonishments of the Lord to them, they were blind; they had forgotten what the word humility even meant. They neglected the self introspection of their own hearts in the asking of God to speak and to reveal their shortcomings and forgive the sin in their own lives, and to know him as Abraham knew him.

If having done this first; in looking to God as Abraham did and not leaving the other things undone, this would have been acceptable to God, even as Jesus had said.

Jesus was addressing the psyche of their obsessive behavior, to wit came their ritual focus and their self inaugurated traditions of the Law. Jesus likened it to idolatry, this very mind-set and practice of tradition-law worship as the worship of God. This is why Jesus referred to them as the blind leading the blind and idolaters in the first place!

This religious system that evolved; with God secondary to the traditions and the Law, is modern Judaism and Catholicism and all the religious groups that are modeled after Catholicism of today. The thought of God speaking and man hearing the Voice of God was as incompatible to them then, as it is to them today. For them there is only the rule by the Law, or rule of Tradition because of this they have killed the Prophets sent to them. Isaiah, Jeremiah, Zachariah, John the Baptist and their Messiah Jesus of Nazareth and thereafter those that carried the testimony of Jesus, and that is, God speaks to me because he is risen and I believe. They of both accounts, the Rabbinical clerics and Catholic autocrats, have continually persecuted those who believed after the order of the way of Melchizedek and that is, God speaks, and I hear.

God had called these people to be a peculiar people different from the rest of the world. By their lip-service which they feign to the Living God and their fanaticism to their tradition of rule by Law worship, they have become no different in their ways than any other religion. In that they commemorate and worship and trust in a "system" for salvation, instead of the "Living God," they have become exactly the same as the Egyptians of before that had persecuted them or any other religion past or present. With their endless repetitions, whether they are banging their heads on the Wailing Wall or saying the rosary, it is all the same! A futile means of showing their faithful devotion to a system and commemoration of those things that they both claim to honor, the same Prophets, Apostles and Saints their ancestors killed are now given incessant lip-service, saying these are our heroes.

God is the God of the living, he is not a mythology as the mind of the unbelieving man is continually directed his fellow man to believe. It is this molding of man's mind with the concept of God as an object of commemoration of the historical past, and the following of observances and sacred rituals whether Jewish or ancient Egyptian, Moslem, or Hindu, Buddhist or Zoroastrian or any of the many Christian creeds, which also give lip-service to the Living God but yet practice a tradition of "creed worship". It is this idea that these systems of worship will lead to eternal life are but a cruel snare, a mocking game. Guess the right system and you live; guess wrong, too bad, you die! This is the system of the world and the meaning of the catch-phrase (being of the world). This system is a cruel and cynical game orchestrated by a cruel and cynical being. Who mocks all those on earth and he has made it his career. "I hope you guess his name," Mr. Mick Jagger knows.

This was not the way of Abraham. Abraham did not look to the past, but to the contrary he followed the Voice from heaven as did Isaac and Jacob and Joseph, even Moses, who gave the Law. Even as David and Isaiah and Daniel, now these were peculiar people who heard the Voice of God and walked with him. These others of whom it is written which walked not by the voice of God it says in the scriptures:

> This is the rest where in you shall cause the weary to find rest. This is the refreshing, yet they would not hear. But the word of the Lord was to them precept upon precept upon precept. and Line upon line upon line: Here a little there a little: That they might go

> and fall backwards and be broken and taken and snared. Isaiah 28:12-13

With the event of the crucifixion of Jesus of Nazareth the world of the descendants of Jacob were split into two main factions, those that accepted Jesus of Nazareth as the promised Messiah and those that rejected him as a heretic. At this time in history early Christians were perceived as one of the many sects within the Jewish community, by both Rome and the rest of the world alike. Yet these early Christians were different, they followed God as a Living God. This was a greater threat to the authorities at Jerusalem than when Jesus was teaching in their synagogues and temple. God would speak to them and they would do, even as it is recorded in the book of "Acts of the Apostles." Stephen with his vision of heaven at his execution in Jerusalem at the hands of the Sanhedrin, also Philip by faith, arose and traveled to Gaza by the voice of God when the Holy Spirit spoke and said "Go from Jerusalem to Gaza," so Philip arose and went. There was also a man named Ananias of Damascus, and the Lord said to him:

> "Ananias arise and go into the street which is called straight and inquire in the house of Judas for one called Saul of Tarsus for behold he is praying. For he has seen in a vision a man named Ananias coming in and putting his hand on him that he receive his sight."

Then this man Ananias said,

> "Lord I have heard many things of this man. He has done much evil to your saints at Jerusalem and he has been given authority from the chief Priest to capture all that call Upon you my Lord."

But the Lord said,

> "Be on your way: For he is a chosen vessel to be a

witness of me to the Gentiles, and kings and the children of Israel. For I will show him how great things he must suffer for me and my namesake."

Ananias went his way, and entered into the house and putting his hands on Saul and said:

"Brother Saul the Lord Jesus who appeared to you in the way has sent me that you receive your sight and be filled with the Holy Ghost." Acts 9:

This same man Saul became known as Paul and God dealt with him the same way as he dealt with Ananias and Philip. None of these men looked to other men for a confirmation or as an intermediary between them and God. They did what they did ready to stand before God for what they did. This is the true meaning of <u>faith</u>. Faith comes by hearing HIM! Even as Peter had to move by faith when he received the vision of a great sheet coming down from heaven filled with every kind of animal in it and God said: "Eat." This was against the Jewish dietary Law and Peter said: "Not so Lord I have never eaten unclean things." But God said, "That what I have made clean do not call unclean." Peter only had his faith that this was the Voice of the Living God that was speaking to him, for what was said to him was contrary to the Law of Moses. He only had his faith, and he entered the house of Cornelius even though it was forbidden by the Law of Moses, and he witnessed the coming of Christ to the Gentiles. This is the same way as Abraham walked with God, and Isaac and Jacob as well. All these people are definitive examples for all who seek the knowledge of God. Seek his PERSON. God is not found by placing other men above you to hear his voice for you or by building philosophies around someone else's experience. All these men of faith are only simple examples for all to see what faith in God is, they are not rulers over you. They are your examples and God is your heritage.

Even while these men of faith, Peter, Philip, Ananias, Paul, Stephen, and on and on as many as have known God in this way; even while they were yet with us, there were those that didn't

The Way

comprehend. Men of philosophy that did not know the Spirit and could only rationalize God with their natural mind. These brought in arguments from every conceivable aspect, from the trinity doctrine to baptism to circumcision and nearly every other issue and argument that could be possibly made. These men of philosophy were building an image of God so they might worship their image of their natural understanding. These gathered disciples to themselves among the congregation as many as they could gather as blind as they were, the blind ruling the blind. The Apostles found themselves not received and unwelcome by a majority of people within some congregations. In some cases in congregations they had first brought the witness of Christ, too.

> For I know this, that after my departure shall grievous wolves enter in among you, not sparing the flock. Also of your own selves shall men arise speaking contrary things, to draw away disciples after them.
> Paul   Acts 20:29-30

CHAPTER 8

The Dragon's Flood

By the time of 300 A.D. there were over fifty Gnostic sects alone and numerous other sects as well within the Christian community. There were Differing varieties of Jacobites (Jewish Christians) with differing views of Mosaic Law. Many congregations had mixtures of all the above even in the time of the Apostle John, as his letters to the seven Churches of Asia in Book of Revelations of Jesus Christ testifies to. Rev 2:1-20

By the time of Emperor Constantine's beginnings of power, at approximately 300 A.D. the areas of the Roman Empire under his control, Christians were tolerated even employed. While in the eastern parts of the empire, under Diocletian's control, Christians suffered their worst persecutions yet.

Two Christians in particular in Constantine's employment were Lacatius and Eusebus. Lacatius was the tutor of Constantine's children and a bishop in the church. Eusebus was a student of philosophy, as well as being known as the one who interpreted dreams and omens for the emperor. He was given the title of Bishop of Nicomedia, {Nicopolis) the imperial residence of the Emperor. It is this bishop who saw Constantine as a holy warrior, a deliverer, as a prophesied King David, and interpreted Constantine's dreams to reflect the same, by reason of Constantine's tolerance of the Christians within his domain. It is this bishop and his closest allies within the church that authorized and introduced the induction of church members into Constantine's legions, for the liberation of Christians under the domain of Diocletian in the eastern half of the empire. With the pretence of the establishment of the Kingdom of God on earth under the banner of the cross "by this sign conqueror" as Eusebus had interpreted a vision that Constantine had. This was an abrupt shift of consciousness imposed on the church by these two bishops. Constantine was now the patron of these bishops in their attempt to fulfill the scriptures. They took on a completely opposite consciousness from that of Jesus Christ, and what he had expressed in his teaching of non-violence, even as Jesus had testified too, at his trial before Pontius Pilate.

> My kingdom is not of this world. If my kingdom were of this world, then would my servants fight that I should not be delivered to the Jews. But now is my kingdom not from this world. St. John 18:36.

Before this time no one in the congregations ever endorsed war as a means of spreading Jesus' message, or thought to use armed force on believers with differing understandings of their application of faith. Such an act was unthinkable!

In 325 A.D. Constantine the Great, now emperor of all the empire was proclaimed the protector of the faith by these bishops with whom he entered into treaties with at his palace at Nicomedia. He, Constantine, issued a proclamation. The assembling of all the bishops of the church, which numbered eighteen hundred at that time, to meet at Nicea. Yet only about three hundred attended. Constantine insisted on a unified doctrine of faith throughout the empire. With the support of the bishops of his previous agreements at Nicomedia, they set forth the mandate of a universal creed for all called Christians to adhere to. It is suspected that not more than a third of the eighteen hundred bishops in those times ever ratified this document. In the ratification of the Nicean creed of 325 A.D. special rights were afforded these bishops, elevating the bishops above all other disciples except for the emperor. The bishops could only be brought up on a charge in a court of law by his peers from within the newly formed college of bishops. The emperor had the authority to absolve any bishop in criminal or civil matters at his own discretion. All ratifying bishops were, as one would say, grandfathered, into their office. All subsequent bishops were elected by the college of bishops and then approved by the emperor and appointed to their office and diocese.

The church's administration had now shifted twice from its first beginnings, from a benevolent ecclesiastical democracy in its very early stages, as the Apostle's had instructed the congregations to choose amongst themselves the officers of the church. Then to an ecclesiastical republic and the development of the primacy of the bishops and archbishops, and then again to an imperial autocracy headed by Constantine. Now rings true the prophecies of Isaiah and Ezekiel on pages 82 & 83 of this book.

Constantine received the title of Pontiff and was elevated to a place of equality with the twelve Apostles of Jesus Christ even while he was still practicing the worship of the pagan god Apollo. Also among his powers ceded to him by the bishops in attendance at Nicea was the authority to forbid receiving of the oblation of the body and blood of Christ, the Communion, to anyone in the church, and the power of excommunication. The Nicean Creed or the Tradition of the Apostles as it was named by the ratifying bishops, was ratified by a minority that were in the church at this time. This is also the beginning of armed aggression against the dissenting bishops, and their removal from the congregations, if they opposed the new order within the church. More Christians suffered persecution and death under this new order than under all other Roman Emperors prior to this time combined. The priesthood of Melchizedek having endured persecution in the past was now enduring persecution from the new autocratic movement from within, from the ratifiers of the Nicean council, with the sword of Constantine as their enforcer.

The very priesthood of Melchizedek that had raised the church from out of the dust of the earth now moved like a ghost as it had in the past exemplified by the likes of Philip, Ananias, Paul, John, Peter, Stephen, and Abraham Isaac and Jacob, Joseph, Jeremiah and Isaiah, of old times. The prime example of this is Peter's confession and Jesus' proclamation: When Jesus asked the disciples, "Who do men say I am?" and the Apostles said, "Some say you're John the Baptist, some say Elijah, and others say Jeremiah or one of the other prophets." He said, "But who do you say I am?" Peter answered and said, "You are the Christ, the son of the Living God." Then, Jesus said to Simon:

> Blessed are you Simon, for flesh and blood has not revealed this to you but my Father that is in heaven. I say also to you, you are Peter and on this rock I will build my church and the gates of hell shall not prevail against it.

The rock was not Simon the man, or was it the revelation of Jesus being the Promised Christ; in the sense of the word of that revelation itself as a noun. The rock on which Christ is building his church is the revealing of revelation by the Father. The very sense of the verb My Father is revealing I am the Christ. This is the rock of Jesus that the gates of hell will not prevail over. It is the following of the living Word of God from heaven as the examples mentioned above lived their lives!

This priesthood of Melchizedek exists on the earth today as it did at the birth of the Church, even as it did in the times of the great prophets like Isaiah. Always enduring the persecutions of fallen man and always leaving a testimony of God as a witness to those generations which persecuted it. So has it been down through history to this present day.

> The wind blows where it pleases, and you hear its sound; but you do not know whence it comes or whether it goes; So is everyone who is born of the Spirit. Jesus

The bishops who conspired with Constantine in establishing this new order were men, not born of the spirit with non-regenerated minds. They willfully went in opposition of the teaching of Jesus Christ; they proved their seed, as Christ foretold they would.

> These things I have spoken to you so that you do not stumble. For they will put you out of the places of worship; and the hour will come that those that kill you will think that they do God's service. These things will they do to you, because they Have not known my father or me. Jesus St. John 16: 1-2

He left his parables as a sort of dictionary to define and identify the nature of the beast, and the nature of God. One such parable is as follows:

> The kingdom of heaven is like a man who sowed good seed in his field. But when the man slept, his enemy came and sowed thorns among the wheat. Then went away. But when the blades of wheat sprang up and bore fruit the thorns appeared also. So the workers of the landowner came and said to him. Behold the field. Where have these thorns come from? The landowner said to his workers: My enemy did this. His workers then said to him. Sir do you want us to go and pull out the thorns? But the landowner said: no it might be while pulling out the thorns you will uproot my wheat also. Let them both grow together until the harvest. At the harvest season, I will say to the reapers, gather out the thorns first and bind them into bundles to be burned. Then gather the wheat into my barn.

Then his disciples asked Jesus to explain the meaning of his parables. He answered and said:

> He who sowed the good seed is the Son of Man. The field is the world: the good seed are the children of the kingdom: but the thorns are the children of evil. The enemy who sowed the thorns is Satan. The harvest is the end of the world: and the reapers are the angels. As the thorns are gathered and burned in

> fire: So shall it be at the end of this world. The Son of Man will send forth his angels and they will gather out of his kingdom all things that offend and them that do iniquity: They will be cast into a furnace of fire, there shall be weeping and gnashing of teeth. Then will the righteous ones shine like the sun in the kingdom of their father. He who has ears to hear let him hear. Matthew 13: 37-43.

This is the wisdom of the Lord. Now what is the sign of Faith? If the autocrats of Nicea believed in the God they profess, they would have never started the persecution of the dissenting bishops of the Nicean counsel with the accusations and distorted interpretations of their views on matters of faith, even if some of them may have been incorrect in their teaching of the gospel. With these feigned motives the Nicean autocrats have been hunting those that are born of the Spirit for the last one thousand six hundred and seventy seven years. Their witness against anyone is dubious at best.

The Spanish inquisition of a mere five hundred years ago testifies to their commitment that no one is to refute the Nicean creed "The Tradition of the Apostles." Herein are their motives revealed. That they are following these traditions and these traditions are to have precedents over the Voice of God by the disallowance of revelation among the congregations.

Of a truth the Holy Scriptures are a written witness of those who have heard the voice of God. But the Holy Scriptures are not the end of God's revelation but only the beginning, the beginning of the voice of God to those who believe. Many want you to believe God's revelation was finished with the canonization of the scriptures, and mankind is to follow the scriptures as the priests or clergy interpret them with humility, in the tradition of whatever denomination one is associated with, as do Jews with the Torah and Mishna and as do Muslims with the Koran. In accepting their interpretation you follow their tradition of God. God is then to you as with them a mythology after the manner of men, like all religions of the past. Whether the Apostles Creed of Nicea or the mythology of Egypt or Islam, in this case they all have become the same thing.

The doctrine of Satan is: God does not speak to people individually anymore. The doctrine of Satan is the blasphemy of the Holy Ghost. What father would prefer that his children, his sons and daughters learn of him from a book, and never come to know him in person?

Those that build their house on tradition build on sand, and great will be their fall, for they build on the interpretation of others and do not know the Voice of God for themselves. Jesus said:

> Beware of false prophets, which come to you in sheep's clothing but inwardly they are ravenous wolves. Ye shall know them by their fruits. Do men gather grapes from thorns, or figs from thistles? Even so every good tree brings forth good fruit. But a corrupt tree brings forth evil fruit. A good tree cannot bring forth evil fruit neither can a corrupt tree bring forth good fruit. Every tree that brings not good fruit is cut down and cast into the fire. Whereby their fruits ye shall know them.
>
> Not everyone that says to me Lord Lord shall enter the kingdom of Heaven: but he that does the will of my Father who is in heaven. Many will say to me Lord Lord have we not preached in your name? And in your name cast out demons and in your name done many great works.
>
> Then will I profess to them I never knew you. Depart from me you that work iniquity.

The Apostle Paul told the congregation at Corinth they had missed the high mark, the high calling in Christ. When there arose arguments within the church whether to follow Paul or whether to follow Apollas, a Greek convert and co-worker with Paul, he told them they are still carnal in their thought and walk as men. He told them I may plant and another may water but it is God revealing that gives you your increase.

For three years before his final farewell in chains, Paul warned of the coming of these wolves. The apostle Peter also warned of the wolves, saying:

> With feigned words they will seek to make merchandise of the people. These will deny the Lord that redeemed (bought) them.

If you were famous, one could study many things known about you through research, to the point they knew more about you than some of your own personal friends. But this would not get them an invitation to your wedding. Knowing all about someone is no substitute for being personally acquainted with someone as their friend.

I watch the Paparazzi of today as they follow the rich and famous trying to take pictures of them so they might sell a story to the public, at the expense of another's privacy, simply to make money. I see these people as a proverb and a sign of the times that we live in.

If such a stranger was found to have smuggled themselves into your wedding party uninvited taking pictures to sell to the public what would you want done with them?

What would be your reaction when these interlopers claimed the exclusive rights to disseminate the details of your wedding to the public? Only after they had assassinated those you had chosen to go out into the public on your behalf and invite as many as would come to meet you personally, and share in the joy of your marriage. So all the public that desired would know the details of your wedding as you had planned. How would you react when these who smuggled themselves into your wedding attempted to deny you the dissemination of the facts of your own wedding only so they could make money; how would you feel?

How could such teachers deny the Lord before a congregation to make merchandise of the same? How? By intimidation that there is no other dissemination of facts except the one they dictate to you, and then imposing those views upon the public with fear, and that the consequence of dissention is excommunication, torture and death and banishment to Hell.

Paul writes in his letter to the church at Collossae, saying these things:

> Let no man beguile you of your reward in voluntary submission worshipping (following) of angels (messengers, Priest – Pastors – Bishops, etc.) intruding into those things which they have not seen except with their carnal (natural) minds. Instead of you beholding the head (Christ's living word) from which all the body is joined by joints and bands having its nourishment increase with the increase of God.

These coming schisms were foreseen and foretold by both Jesus and his Apostles, and the parable of the wedding feast in the Gospel of Matthew shows the outcome of those that smuggle themselves improperly dressed to his wedding. Mat 22:1-14

CHAPTER 9

The Wilderness and Time

I write a profound truth, and this is: The church administration set up by the Apostles, in the Book of the Acts of the Apostles of the New Testament of the Bible, does not exist on the earth anymore.

It has been ravaged by the wolves and has not been spared. Just as the Apostles said, it would happen. The flock is scattered and the Shepard's the true Shepard's are hunted from within as well as from without. There are no men on earth that can restore the church for it is not meant to be restored; only at the return of Jesus Christ will she emerge from her place in the wilderness again. There have been movements of God and will be more. They shall come and go like ghosts, they will appear for a season then the wolves will come to dictate and regulate and subjugate, just as it has been. The true church is where the carnal mind is not. The church of Jesus Christ is where man's hand has not reached and that alter is made from uncut stone that no tool of man has polluted. It is where the hand of man cannot go. Wilderness means a place without human administration. Many a man and woman of God from every denomination that encompasses the earth have felt the pressure of the wolves' teeth. There is no restoration of the administration of the church, only of souls. Every denomination that models itself after the concept of the Nicean Creed, and discourages the Father revealing in the congregation or seeks to manage the movement of the Holy Ghost is an opponent of God.

God is a spirit and they that worship him must worship him in spirit and truth. It is deep deep in the heart where the wilderness is, that place which God has prepared for each of us. It is as he that has the keys of David has said:

> I open doors that no man can shut I shut doors that
> no man can open. Rev 3:7

In the coming prophecies in the book of Revelations that we are about to examine there are many sequential numbers. These numbers are of profound significance they confirm the ongoing message of the New Testament Apostles with the ancient order of the way of Melchizedek. They show the same knowledge and astronomical calculations and understandings that have been displayed in the earlier pages of this book. This will show the Apostles concept in regard to the Most High God is after the Order of the way of Melchizedek in all of their ways, and they are the continuation of the Order of Melchizedek. I am a witness they received this knowledge by revelation from the Most High and not by commemoration of traditions or in the study of either Astrology or Astronomy even though both are evidently present. This is the separating factor between those that follow the Voice of the Most High and those that follow the teachings of "men" even when these teachings of men had their knowledge originate with the Most High from the start.

> And there appeared a great sign in heaven: a woman clothed with the sun and the moon under her feet, and upon her head a crown of twelve stars: and she being with child cried, travailing in birth, and pained to be delivered. There appeared another sign in heaven: and behold a great red dragon having seven heads and ten horns, and seven crowns upon his heads.
> And his tail drew the third part of the stars of

The Wilderness and Time

heaven and did cast them to the earth: and the dragon stood before the woman. That was ready to be delivered. For to devour her child as soon as it was born. She brought forth a man child who was to rule all nations with a rod of iron: and her child was caught up unto God and his throne. And the woman fled into the wilderness where she hath a place prepared of God that they should feed her a thousand two hundred and threescore days.

And there was war in heaven: Michael and his angels fought against the dragon: and the dragon fought and his angels and they prevailed not: neither was their place found any more in heaven. The great dragon was cast out that old serpent, called the Devil and Satan, which deceives the whole world: he was cast out onto the earth and his angels were cast out with him. Then I heard a loud voice saying in heaven.

Now is come salvation, and strength, and the kingdom of our God, And the power of his Christ: for the accuser of our brethren is cast down which accused them before our God day and night.

And they overcame him by the blood of the lamb with the word of their testimony: for they loved not their lives unto the death.

Therefore rejoice ye heavens and you that dwell in them. Woe to the inhabitants of the earth and the sea! For the devil is come down unto you, having great wrath, because he knows his time is short.

When the dragon saw that he was cast unto the earth, he persecuted the woman that brought forth the man child. But to the woman were given two wings of a great eagle, that she might fly into the wilderness, into her place where she is nourished for a times time and half a time, from the face of the serpent.

Yet the serpent cast out of his mouth water as a flood after the woman that he might cause her to be

> carried away with the flood. Then the earth helped the woman and the earth opened her mouth and swallowed the flood which the dragon cast out of his mouth.
>
> Now the dragon was enraged with the woman and went to make war with the remnant of her seed, which keep the commandment of God having the testimony of Jesus Christ. Rev: 12.

The numbers in these scriptures are both symbolic and literal but not necessarily as they seem. They denote hidden meaning and can yet tell the numbers they represent; here are some examples and at the completion of these explanations you shall see four different numbers all denoting the same time, or, better put, they all represent the same particular dispensation of time.

Let's start by looking at some unique references in the Gospel of Luke and Revelations to explain the meaning of these numbers.

In Luke 21:24 it says:

> They shall fall by the edge of the sword and shall be led away captive into all nations: and Jerusalem shall be trodden down of the Gentiles, until the times of the Gentiles is fulfilled.

Accepting the notion this passage is in reference to the Diaspora of the Jews at the hand of the Romans in 70 A.D. and the condition of Jerusalem thereafter. We will go on now lets look at Revelations 11:1-4

> There was given me a reed like unto a rod and the angel stood saying. Rise and measure the temple of God, and the altar and them that worship therein.
>
> But the court which is outside the temple leave it out and measure it not: for it is given unto the Gentiles with the Holy city and they shall tread them underfoot forty and two months.
>
> Then I will give unto my two witnesses power;

> and they shall prophesy a thousand two hundred and threescore days clothed in sackcloth. These are the two olive trees, and the two candlesticks standing before the God of the earth.

At first look these two passages seem to contradict each other if you are to take them at face value. One is saying Jerusalem will be trodden underfoot by the Gentiles until the time of the Gentiles is fulfilled, and the other says Jerusalem shall be trodden underfoot by the Gentiles for forty-two months. But actually, they say the same thing. To bring the two together and discover the symbolic meaning of forty two months in this passage of Revelations we need only to remind ourselves that Jerusalem is still, to this day, trodden underfoot by Gentiles, even as it has been since the time of the Diaspora.

But the meaning of this number does begin to unfold in the first chapter of the Gospel of Matthew. Matthew 1:17. It reads:

> So all the generations from Abraham to David are fourteen generations: and from David until the carrying away into Babylon are fourteen generations and from them carrying away into Babylon unto Christ are fourteen generations.

So from the beginning of the promise to the man Abraham, to its completion of the promise with the birth of Jesus of Nazareth the Christ it is forty two generations. Fourteen times three equals forty two. It is also true the number forty-two was the number of the complete body of Egyptian gods in their mythology at one's Day of Judgment. This number forty-two contained the same meaning to both, a number with a symbolic meaning of completion.

Also six, the number or day of man, as man he was created on the sixth day. Times seven the number of days to God's rest for on the seventh day He rested. This too makes forty two. It also makes Jesus Christ himself the Sabbath and the Lord of it.

> Come unto me all you that labor and are heavy laden and I will give you rest. Mt. 11:28.

So the prophetic statement of Jesus, in the Gospel of Luke that Jerusalem shall be trodden underfoot by the Gentiles until the time of the Gentiles is fulfilled and is the foundation statement, John's vision in the book Revelations is harmonized with Jesus' foundation statement by understanding the forty-two months spoken of by John is the full time of the dispensation of the Gentiles.

It is not a literal time of forty-two months according to men, it is symbolic of completion of time: the time of the Gentiles according to Jesus. Also, if one calculates a month's time as thirty days, then times that by forty-two you arrive at one thousand two hundred and sixty days. This number's meaning from Rev. 11:3 is also symbolic of the completion of a dispensation of time in itself. All these numbers are the same, and both sets of numbers are linked to the completion of the dispensation of the time of the Gentiles.

So what is that, you ask? Paul writes in several different letters to the church of this dispensation of the time of Gentiles. First in the letter to the Romans. Romans 11:25:

> For I would not brethren, that you be ignorant concerning this mystery, lest you should become wise in your own conceits that blindness in part is happened to the (Jewish people) Israel, until the fullness of the Gentiles comes in.

Then again in the letter to the church of Ephesus he writes in the 10th verse of the 1st chapter:

> That in the dispensation of the fullness of time he might gather together in one all things in Christ both which are in heaven and on earth even in him.

Then one more of many in the letter to the church of the Galatians. Galatians 4:4

> But when the <u>fullness of time</u> was come God sent forth his Son made of a woman made <u>under the Law</u>.

The Wilderness and Time

Now this verse exemplifies the forty-two generations in itself, as the "fullness of time." So what is a Gentile? The word Gentile is synonymous with the uncircumcised people of the world. When God made his promise to Abraham that this man's offspring after him would inherit and possesses a Promised Land, and that God's covenant was with him and his offspring. Abraham asked the Lord saying: "How will I know I shall inherit all this?" God answered Abraham with an instruction as his explanation; "Take a heifer of three years old and a she-goat of three years old and a ram of three years old and a turtledove and a pigeon."

When Abram took all these animals as the Lord instructed him, the heifer and the she-goat and the ram, he divided them into halves and laid the pieces end to end making eight pieces in all of the five animals for the turtledove and the pigeon he did not cut in half. Then in the space of time there came carrion birds to devour the instructions that Abram had laid out as Lord had told him to do, and Abram drove the birds away keeping watch over the offering the Lord had instructed him to make. When night had fallen, Abram fell asleep and dreamed a nightmare where he saw his descendants afflicted by strangers in a strange land, and God judged their afflicters and delivered the descendants of Abram with great substance, after four hundred years time to the forth generation. Then in the dream God told Abram he would live a good long life and go to his fathers' in peace. Then in the midst of the darkness a burning lamp came as a smoking furnace and passed between the divided heifer, she-goat and ram and the turtledove and pigeon, lighting up the offering. That day the Lord gave Abram all the land between the Nile and the Euphrates rivers.

When Abram was ninety nine years old, the Lord appeared to him again and said:

> I am, Almighty GOD walk before me and be perfect. I make my covenant between me and you and I will multiply you exceedingly. As for me behold my covenant is with you. You shall be the father of many nations. No more will you be called Abram. Your name shall be Abraham: The father of many

> nations. With you I make the everlasting covenant. You shall circumcise the foreskin of every man child at the age of <u>eight days</u>. Those that are your seed and those bought with a price all that is in your household. This will be the <u>symbol (token) the sign</u> of my everlasting covenant with you and your seed to come. The <u>sign</u> of my everlasting covenant will be in your flesh. The uncircumcised man whose flesh of his foreskin is not circumcised that soul will be cut off from his people. For he has broken my covenant.

This is the explanation of what a Gentile is, any one not circumcised. If circumcision is the <u>sign</u> of, or the <u>promise</u> of the everlasting covenant, but not the everlasting covenant itself, what is? This act of circumcision was and is the prophecy of this everlasting covenant. The very voice of God in man, and God leading all people, this is the embodiment of the message of Jesus of Nazareth the Christ and has been inaugurated with his life. This is what all the prophets proclaimed. The writer of Hebrews describes the Voice this way:

> The word of God is <u>living</u> and powerful it is sharper than any two edged sword, piercing even to the point of division between soul and spirit and between the joints and marrow and bones, it is a discerner of the thoughts and intents of the heart. There is no creature hidden from his sight; All things are naked and open before the eyes of him who we must answer to. Heb: 4:12-13

It is the following of this the unction of all truth the Voice of the Living God coming forth in us, in all his glory lighting up the five senses of our natural minds, with the mind of God Almighty. This is the burning lamp as a smoking furnace passing between the heifer, the she-goat, the ram, the turtledove and the young pigeon. This is the new week or the 8th day. This is the everlasting covenant this is the distinction between the circumcised and the uncircumcised.

The crucifixion of Jesus of Nazareth was the payment and

inauguration of this everlasting covenant with God sending his Holy Spirit.

This is how the city and the outer court could be trodden underfoot by the Gentiles for forty two months. But the Temple and those that worship inside at its altar are untouched. This is also the same place where the woman that brought forth the man child now rests for the one thousand two hundred and sixty days. These are those that John had numbered, and they are in the temple he measured, but those in whom this work of circumcision is not in process, and this work is not taking place within them, they are without. They are not numbered with those that worship in this Temple, they are the cut off. It is Jesus that holds the keys of David, He alone opens doors that no man can shut and shut doors that no man can open. This now quantifies the statement that Jesus makes. Jerusalem would be trodden underfoot by the Gentiles until the time of the Gentiles is fulfilled and the vision of John and those that worship in this Temple.

It is this time of the Gentiles, that is also the time and dispensation of the preaching of the Gospel of Jesus Christ, and his kingdom to the Gentiles that is spoken by all the Apostles and St. John in Revelation 11:3

> I will give authority to my two witnesses, and they will prophesy a thousand two hundred and sixty days in sackcloth

Speaking of these two witnesses in sackcloth; in the time of the ancients when a king or priest whose conscience was pricked by the voice of God to repentance, that king or priest would remove his clothes and put on sackcloth, commoners clothes, and go before God with his supplications and vow his repentance in the sight of God and return to following God. Sackcloth has nothing to do with poverty or vagabonds and beggars or how one is dressed in this the natural world as some might have others believe. It is a state of being, in ones own heart, the humbling of oneself in the presence of the Lord and the following of his truth, knowing he loves those he corrects now in the window of this dispensation of time.

Now to continue on in the book of Revelation 11:4. It says:

> These are the two olive trees and the two candlesticks standing before the God of the earth.

Consider what has been spoken of earlier, concerning the alignments of the Sphinx with Bethlehem and Mt. Sinai in the earlier chapters of this book and the titles and names given to the Sphinx. Let's examine these alignments of the summer solstice and Bethlehem, and the winter solstice and Mt. Sinai. I can think of no more glorious example on this earth and in this physical realm, of two candlesticks, than the sun rising over the horizon with these two monumental places of time and them being within the disc of the rising sun as a definition of candlesticks.

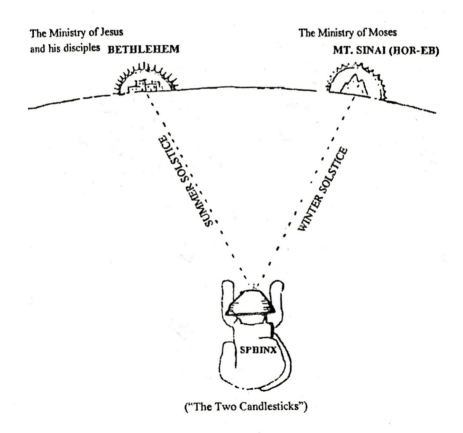

("The Two Candlesticks")

The Wilderness and Time

In ancient times the language of the science of Astronomy was universally expressed in Astrological terminology regardless of one's loyalty to their faith. It is time the Christian community as a whole began looking at the zodiac in an Astronomical rather than an Astrological perception instead of the enemy where Astronomy is concerned. It is just another language in this instance. To fail to do so will leave the modern Christian superstitiously ignorant and as willfully belligerent, as the Roman Catholic Church in the middle Ages, actually the Dark Ages. When people risked their lives over such issues from one's confession of faith that God spoke to him or her or whether the earth was round or flat. The Roman Catholic Church needed to suppress the truth and keep the masses uneducated to propagate their perverted religious system, and they did so with all their strength.

The Apostle Paul writes to the Christians in Rome in the first century A.D. around the time of Emperor Nero. He wrote:

> For the wrath of God is revealed from heaven against all the iniquity and wickedness of unjust men who suppress the truth. Because that which may be known God was manifested to them, for God had revealed it to them. For the invisible things of him from the creation of the world are clearly seen, being understood by the things that are made even his eternal power and Godhead: so that they are without excuse:
>
> Because that when they knew God they glorified him not as God neither were they thankful: but they became vain in their own imaginations, and their foolish hearts were darkened. Professing themselves to be wise they became fools. For they changed the glory of the incorruptible God into an image made like corruptible man and to birds, and four footed beasts, and creeping things. For this cause
>
> God also gave them over to uncleanliness, through the lust of their own hearts to dishonor their own bodies between themselves.

> These who changed the truth of God into a lie, and worshipped and served the creation more than the Creator, who is blessed forever.
> Amen:
> Therefore God has given them up to their own vile passions. They even changed their women's natural purpose into that which was unnatural. And also their men have left the natural reason for women, and have burned in their lust toward one another; men with men committing shameful acts, and receiving in themselves the due recompense of their error.
> Even as they did not like to retain God in their knowledge God gave them over to a reprobate mind, to do the things which should not be done but now do. Romans 1:18-28

Also likewise did the Egyptians and the Magi of the east; they too corrupted the truth for vanity and national pride's sake, losing the meaning of their most ancient knowledge and without the voice of God wandered in desolate places, blind and without, they invented myths in place of the truth of the Living Word that they had now come to despise. Even as Cain despised Able, yet the eyes of the wise can still see a thread of truth which is woven in the tapestry of their mythology that they have made for their own covering. But for the most part, concerning the leaders of the Magi, the Prophet Isaiah writes

> Surely the Princes of Zoan have become fools, and the wise counselors of Pharaoh have become vain in their counsel: how is it they say to Pharaoh. You are the son of the wise the son of the ancients.
> Where are they? Where are the wise of old? Let them tell you now, and let them know what the Lord of Hosts proposed for Egypt.
> The Princes of Zoan have become fools. The priests of Memphis have become haughty and have

lead Egypt astray even the foundation of her family. (Pharaoh)

The Lord has allowed a spirit of deceit to enter within her and it has caused the Egyptian to err in all its works, as a drunken man staggers in his vomit. Neither shall there be any leader for Egypt who can make heads nor tails of it, or tails or heads. (of the plan of the Lord of Hosts)

On that day Egypt shall be like a woman, and he shall be afraid and tremble because of the shaking of the hand of The Lord of Hosts, which he shakes against him.

The land of Judah shall be a terror to the Egyptian. Everyone who makes mention of it shall be filled with dread because of the counsel of the Lord of Hosts which he has determined against the Egypt.

In that day there shall be five cities in the land of Egypt which will speak the language of Canaan and swear by the Lord of Hosts: one of them shall be called Haris, the city of destruction.

On that day there shall be an altar to the Lord in the midst of the land of Egypt, and a pillar at its borders to the Lord. It shall be a sign and a witness to the Lord of Hosts in the land of Egypt: for they shall cry to the Lord because of the oppressor, and he shall send them a savior and judge and he shall deliver them.

The Lord shall be known to the Egyptians, and the Egyptians shall know the Lord in that day, and shall acknowledge his sacrifice and obligation. Yes, they shall vow a vow to the Lord and keep it. The Lord shall smite the Egyptians; he shall smite and heal them.

In that day there shall be a highway from Egypt to Assyria and from Assyria to Egypt and Assyrians shall come into Egypt and the Egyptian into Assyria and the Egyptians shall serve the Assyrians. In that day Israel shall be the third with Egypt and with Assyria, even a blessing in the midst of the land. Whom The Lord of Hosts shall bless saying blessed be Egypt my people, and Assyria the work of my hands, and Israel my heritage. Isaiah 19:11-25.

This biblical quotation from Isaiah is but one of the many subtle hints anthropologically speaking, that suggests the Assyrians (Harranian) had a hand in the construction of the Great Sphinx, the centerpiece of the Giza observatory. This is supported by archaeological evidence as well. Especially when one takes into consideration that sphinxes in general are not considered to have had their origins with Egyptian culture by many scholars. To the contrary many scholars attribute sphinxes origins to early Assyrian type cultures.

To refresh our memory remember that Professor Robert Schoch of Boston University had studied the Sphinx for signs of water erosion of the limestone from which the Sphinx is carved. Also the limestone blocks of the adjoining temple that was quarried from around the Sphinx itself. Dr. Schoch places the date of the Sphinx construction at a minimum age of 6,000 years old at around 4,000 B.C. This is 1,500 years earlier than previously believed. His findings are supported by the majority of the Geological Society of America.

Also remember; in the 1930's and 40's Egyptologist Selim Hassan uncovered a colony of people at Giza that he refers to as Sabians. They were called the Starworshippers by the Ancient Egyptians. Dr. Hassan viewed these people as an archetype of the Magi from the sacred Assyrian city of Harran. Not coincidentally this is where Abraham was from.

Dr. Hassan dates the Sabian colony of Giza as far back as the early second millennium B.C. The Orthodox Egyptologist contributes the building of the Sphinx to the Pharaoh Khafre who reigned from 2520 – 2494 B.C.

Dr. Zahi Hawass, Director General of Giza, in charge of excavations in Egypt, called professor Schoch of Boston University and his colleagues' conclusions "ridiculous, American hallucinations." Dr. Hawass says the sphinx is the soul of Egypt. He has also gone on record repeating what Dr. Hassan had stated that the ancient Egyptian people referred to the Sphinx by its Harranian (Assyrian) name, Hwl.

It is inconceivable that the ancient Egyptians would call what Dr. Hawass describes as the soul of Egypt, by a name that interlopers had given for it. According to Dr. Hassan, these people made pilgrimages to the monument from their country as an object of worship. To the contrary, if the honor and title is given to the builder, these people were highly esteemed and this Assyrian name "Hwl" may point to its builders.

Taking these factors into consideration, along with the immense pride of the ancient Egyptian people, Dr. Zahi Hawass may have inadvertantly attributed this edifice to the early Harranian or Akkadians with cultural, chronological, and linguistic evidence.

Twelve hundred years after the time of Khafre, at the death of Amenhotep IV son Tutankhamen, his wife Ankhsnamum asked the King of Assyria to send her one of his sons to be her husband. Saying none in Egypt were worthy of maintaining the divine bloodline. This implies a connection from antiquity between these two nations. With the fact the ancient Egyptians called the sphinx by its Assyrian name; this gives one pause for thought. At the least there is enough evidence to suggest that the building of the Sphinx was a multinational effort in man's prehistory.

These people from Harran from which sprang the order of the Magi, flourished throughout Mesopotamia, and reached as far as China, but their power base eventually centered in Persia. They continue even to this day integrated into several different religions of Zoroastrianism that we spoke of earlier. To include every group of people who employ Astrology today in one way or another; all have their roots of their practice branching from the Magi.

Again one must ask oneself what did the Magi of Jesus' time have to do with Jesus in the first place. Why would these astrologers seek to pay homage to Jesus? Asking Herod the Great, King of Judea, where is he that is born King of the Jews?

I believe there is no other explanation why, other than the reason I have espoused in this book. With the evidence this priesthood of astronomers and Astrologers had witnessed the sign of the universal King of Kings.

Why didn't Herod parade his own sons in front of them? Why did Herod have to ask the Chief Priest and scribes where is this King of Jews they speak of going to be born? Why would he have to gather all the chief priests and scribes of the people together in counsel to determine from them, where the King of the Jews was to be born? Why didn't he know this off the tip of his tongue, or just be able to lean over his shoulder and whisper to the nearest priest where is the King of the Jews to be born? Unless what the Magi asked was, "Where is the King of Kings for we have seen his star and have come to worship". If this was the case, these Magi saw Jesus as a Universal Messiah and not just Messiah for Jews.

By our time in history most Astrologers of today have come to understand God in their estate, as a God of forces, as a Higher Power, void of an intimate personality. By coming to worship Jesus these Magi were committing heresy by the standards that prevail within astrology of today. The acknowledgement of a personified Messiah is contrary to their philosophy, such beliefs in God as a god of forces always finds justification in itself at the expense of others, no matter how well it is packaged. Even as the prophet Daniel witnessed concerning our time more than 2500 years ago.

This order of the Magi split from the order of Melchizedek, long before the time of the Hebrew Patriarchs. But there are enough shadows of the Messianic order of Melchizedek woven within the tapestry of their early rudimentary beliefs that suggests what has been expounded on with example after example in the pages of this book is creditable

Now as then, people continue in the act of avoiding the voice of God face to face even as Adam and Eve did, by the same beguilement of the serpent as they had, when he promised them the power to be Gods for themselves. But instead they hide themselves from the face of God under the trees of the garden. This is what man does, thinking if they sew enough fig leaves together it will cover

The Wilderness and Time

the nakedness of their rebellion. All religion looks to the observance of tradition and mythology with a hierarchy of priests and mediators over them as a buffer between God and man. This is the meaning of the event when Jesus healed a blind man with his spittle and asked the blind man what he saw, and the blind man said he saw men as trees, and then Jesus touched him again and his sight was made whole Jesus told him to tell no one. Man seeks a consensus from other men in numbers because he is afraid when God calls him by name, this is when man hides. This is the same hiding of Adam under the trees of the garden and Adam (mankind) has come to resent his Creator because he hides from his presence.

The Magi of our time and its Astrologers that interpret the message of the night sky of heaven today, do so with their own observations and interpretation of the stars in place of the Voice of the Creator who made all things so. These are the same wolves that have entered the church many years ago and turned the truth of God into a mythology, a lie after the way of dead men. Today they stand in the estate of the Magi of old, and they shall lead this world, as they lead many of the world rulers already, to throw off the message that God has put in his heavens that is proclaimed by the Order after the way of Melchizedek. They shall trample the message of the personified Messiah under their feet. Even as their counterparts proclaim their "New Age" free of the old superstitions and the final death of the old order after the Order of Melchizedek.

They shall proclaim mankind is his own savior of this earth; even as their Astrologers interpret the new Astrological age the earth is now moving into, as the age of enlightenment.

By now any Bible scholar reading this has come to the conclusion that I do not see a seven year period at the end of this age, known by most Bible scholars and theologians as the Great Tribulation. That is correct. It is also correct for them to assume that I see this period of tribulation to span the entire time of the Gentiles. This also is true.

If there is a seven year tribulation at the end of this age God has hidden it from me. Even though this is what was taught at me in every denomination I have ever entered. While they were debating over the issue of a pre-tribulation rapture or a mid-tribulation rapture or post-tribulation rapture, I couldn't find the truth in what they were all debating over in the first place. As far as the "Dead in Christ" rising first and we who remain joining him in the air (Spirit) or breath as is the designated true meaning in Greek, we will discuss in greater detail near the end of this chapter.

If all these things spoken of in the book of Revelations were to happen literally as they say, in such a short period of time, within seven years, only the most dull-witted of persons the very most dull-witted person could ever miss the coming of Christ. Yet Jesus said he shall come like a thief in the night. (So I sought God for myself to the meaning of all this, only that I may know the truth, and I have shared this with you.) I believe these numbers are symbolic time frames, and not literal at all.

The Apostle John wrote concerning the coming of the Antichrist by which the theologians define the Great Tribulation that they, the Antichrist would come from within the Church! John writes:

> My children it is the last time; and as you were told that Antichrist shall come, even now there are many Antichrist and from this we know that it is the last time. They went out from among us: But they were not of us. For if they had been of us they would have continued with us. But they left us that it might be known they did not belong with us. But you have been anointed by the Holy One and are made able to distinguish between men; (trees)

> As for you, if the anointing which you have received from him abides in you. You need no man to teach you: For this same <u>anointing which is of God will teach you all things</u>. 1 John 2:18-20&27

As concerning the Four Horseman of the Apocalypse, the same is also true; they are a window testifying to the Geo-political state of the world, represented by the description and events accompanying each horseman. I will begin at chapter 6:1 & 2 of Revelations:

> And I saw when the Lamb opened one of the seals I heard as it were the sound of thunder then one of the four creatures from around the Throne of God said to me come and see. Then I saw behold a white horse: and he that sat on the white horse had an archers bow: and a crown was given unto him and he went forth conquering and to conquer.

This horse and his rider represent the time of imperialism that has spanned most of earth's history, the age of far flung empires as depicted by the archers bow and his crown. From Imperial Egypt to the English empire as the mode of world order through time, this gave way in time to the next Geo-political reality but not necessarily all at once.

> And when the Lamb had opened the second seal; I heard the second creature from around the throne of God say to me behold come and see. Then there went forth another horse that was red and power was given to him that sat upon the red horse to take peace from off the earth; and that they should kill one another; and a great sword was given to him.

This horse and his rider is representative of the shot that was heard around the world. With its beginnings the American Revolution of 1776; from this time forward even till now the world has been at war. People have been overthrowing the old orders around the world. Different people declaring independence from each other in every corner of the globe, war without rest in the name of peace and liberty, even as democracy dominates and defines this Geo-political reality now on earth. But this time is waning even as we speak, and it is giving way to the next world order that is to dominate the landscape of the earth.

> And when the Lamb had opened the third seal, I heard the third creature from around the throne of God say: come and see and I beheld lo a black horse

> and he that sat on the black horse had in his hand a pair of scales(balances). Then I heard the voice from within the midst of the four creatures that were around the throne of God say a measure of wheat for a penny and three measures of barley for a penny and see that you do not hurt (interrupt) the wine or the oil.

This third seal speaks of the world plutocracy that will be the subtle substitute for the Democracies of the second seal; this will bring the emergence of the global economic system. Even as it is now coming into being. The scales or balances in the rider's hand is world trade as the dominating factor that will govern the way the planet is managed, a time of prosperity and profit for many, as represented by the color of the horse. In business the thing to be in is the black, and as described by the vision itself, do not interrupt the oil or the wine. This is what is paramount to this system: keeping the oil flowing, keeping the petrol-economy's commerce moving. This time will be shorter than that of the two previous horsemen.

> And when he had opened the fourth seal I heard the voice of the fourth creature say come and see: And I looked and behold a pale horse and his name that sat on him was Death and hell followed with him. And power was given unto them over the fourth part of the earth to kill them with the sword and with hunger and with Death and with the beasts of the earth.

This seal speaks of the outcome of the greed of the third seal as they will pre-empt the civil rights for others to prevent any interruption of supply of goods to the global economy. Greed and envy and resentment will grow and those who want their piece of the global economic pie with feigned leadership from all sides, all of them will make war for profit. In this time shall the complete hatefulness and mischief of man rise to its highest, bringing terrible suffering over a fourth part of the earth, war hunger, pestilences, all the works of unrepentant man, and the fall of the governments of ungodly man. Anyone with even half a heart can see that this vision that John had of these horsemen is the prophetic truth. This is our world we live in today as our history is unfolding before our eyes.

Researchers from Los Alamos Laboratory published a thesis (LA-UR 004608), in this study these researchers developed a model recreating a volcanic eruption of such proportion that it staggers the human mind. This eruption is known as the Proto-Krakatau. It occurred in the year 536 AD in the present day country of Indonesia. This predecessor was many times greater than the 1815 AD eruption of Krakatau of the same name and place. The evidence these scientists have brought forth is that this resulting blast of this super volcano with its caldera or magma chamber collapsing beneath it formed the Strait of Sunda between the islands of Sumatra and Java where prior to this explosive eruption the two islands were one land mass. The bathymetric data indicates this caldera to be about 40 to 60 km in diameter.

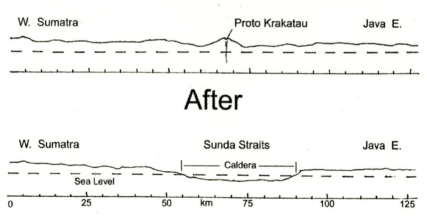

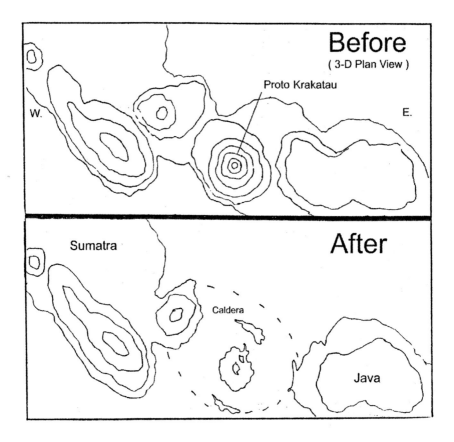

This eruption blew huge amounts of volcanic ash into the Stratosphere. The researchers from Los Alamos Laboratory estimate that as much as 100 km3 of sea water was vaporized as sea water attempted to fill the super heated magma chamber during the eruption. This triggered a secondary explosion greater than the first and this was the most devastating part of the whole eruption. The resulting secondary explosion of sea water coming in contact with magma formed a cloud layer up to 150 meters thick of ice and super fine volcanic ash as high as 50 km into the Stratosphere. This cloud layer engulfed the entire globe. The effects of this would last for nearly a century.

The island was literally blown in half. Sumatra to the west and Java to the east. This is even documented in ancient Indonesian literature though it was thought this was just a legend until recently.

The Wilderness and Time

It is most likely a major contributing factor in the decline of that civilization. The results of this eruption were recorded by all cultures world wide that kept records at that time; the Sun was dimmed and its light was feeble. Snow and darkness were recorded in mid-summer of the same year in China.

The Italian historian Flavius Cassiodorus wrote in 536 A.D.:

> "The sun seems to have lost its wonted light, and appears a bluish color. We marvel to see no shadows of our bodies at noon, or to feel the mighty vigor of the Sun's heat it is wasted into feebleness, and the phenomena which accompanies an eclipse has prolonged through almost the whole year. We have had summer without heat. The crops have been chilled by the north winds, and rain is denied."

Other writers of this time also describe similar conditions:

> Procopius: "During this year a most dreaded portent took place. For the Sun gave forth its light without brightness, and it seem exceedingly like the Sun was in eclipse, for the beams it shed were not clear.

> Michael the Syrian: "The Sun became dark and its darkness has lasted eighteen months. Each day shone for about four hours, and still this light was only a feeble shadow...the fruits did not ripen, and the wine tasted like sour grapes."

Many of these recounts of this time and event were published in the September 1999 issue of "Universe" by Greg Bryant. The work published by Mr. Bryant "The Dark Ages; Were They Darker Than We Imagined?" Has a differing opinion than that of the researchers at Los Alamos to what caused this darkness but neither of the two are incorrect in their conclusions of this world wide catastrophe in 536 A.D.

Bryant gathered information from a college of colleagues

including the following:

-Mike Baillie: Professor of Palaeoecology at Queens University in Belfast, Northern Ireland;

-Marie Agnes Courty: French Archaeologist;

-British Astronomers: Fred Whipple, Mark Bailey, Victor Clube;

-Dr. Brian Marsden: of the Smithsonian Astrophysical Observatory;

-Duncan Steel: former AAO Astronomer and Author;

-Ben Rudders, Anthropologist;

-Bill Napier, Author, "Origin of Comets."

The Bryant scenario deduces at around 400 A.D. the Earth's orbit began to pass through a swarm of comet fragments related to the comet Encke in the Taurid meteor stream. In his work Bryant calculates the Earth passes through the core of this meteor stream that contains the largest and most concentrated fragments of the comet Encke, this intersection takes place every 2,500 years since the comet's break up, and at these times the Earth receives an elevated bombardment of Tunguska-class impacts wiping out thousands of square miles of vegetation and animal life at a time; much like the Tunguska blast of 1908 in Central Siberia. It is these elevated frequencies of bombardments in the compressed period of time of about two hundred years, from 400 A.D. to 600 A.D that Bryant and his colleagues present as their historical scenario. Using Chinese records of the same time period Bryant and his colleagues deduce that Central and East Asia were devastated by a series of impacts that forced mass migrations of whole Asian communities and nations on a westward migration for suitable lands. As they moved west they displaced nation after nation, forcing them westward into the Roman Empire triggering the barbarian invasion that eventually brought the demise of Rome. Bryant and his colleagues surmise that a type of nuclear winter took place over the whole planet thus what has come down to us through history known as the Dark Ages was an accurate description of the world at that time. It was actually dark and most of world political orders collapsed. Out of the devastation of these times rose a new order or new light known as Islam.

Interestingly, science has concluded a comet is made of ice and dust particles like a dirty snow ball flying though space.

At this time you might be saying to yourself: How does this information have anything to do with this book?

This book is written demonstrating a prophetic knowledge of a Living Being, the Creator of all things, and this Being has reserved the pleasure to retain his knowledge and chooses to disseminate his plans for his creation to those he pleases as his witness of himself. It is in those people's testimonies of his knowledge that history itself unfolds, even as his chosen have foretold. It pleases him to reveal his plans to those that are his friends.

Let's look at the book of Revelation. As I have stated earlier, I see this book as a concurrent revelation rather than so much as a lineal revelation as demonstrated with the four Horsemen of the Apocalypse as representations of the historical world governments from the beginning of time to the present and of what is still yet to come. I see this rather than just prophesied events that are to happen in the future at the end of time. Also because of the reoccurring use of the numbers forty-two and one thousand, two hundred sixty: With their association with the completion of time also compels me to look at this concurrently instead of adding these individual numbers together concerning their stated events to produce what others called the "Seven Year Tribulation" at the end of time which is commonly espoused by most who study this subject. This concurrent theme is what is testified to throughout the book of Revelations with our own history as its witness. When John saw the vision of the Beast he is told they are Kings: five are fallen, one is and one is yet to come, and the Beast itself (that is the entire system) is the eighth and that goes into perdition. This concurrent consciousness is repeated over and over through that book. So, to ascribe that book to the last seven years of time is folly.

> I am the Alpha and Omega, the beginning and the ending says The Lord, which is and which was, and which is to come, the Almighty. Rev. 1:8

After the four Horsemen in the beginning of chapter six, the book of Revelation is a macro view of the mechanics of his creation in heaven from the time of his earliest followers through to the coming darkness of the great falling away up to the wobble of the earth and the judgment of the nations as prophesied by Isaiah, Daniel and John. All this can be read in the latter parts of Revelation's chapter six. Chapters seven and eight go into greater details of the events of latter parts of chapter six; that was, that were and what were yet to come.

> And the seven angels which had the seven trumpets prepared themselves to sound. The first angel sounded, and there followed hail and fire mingled with blood and it was cast upon the earth: and a third part of the trees was burnt up and all the green grass was burnt up. Rev.8: 6-7

This is an uncanny accurate description of the bombardment of the earth as the earth passed through the core of the fragments of the comet Encke in the Taurid meteor stream beginning around 400 A.D. The description of hail mingled with fire is an exactly defined explanation of comet fragments impacting on the earth. The subsequent dislocation of masses of Asian people migrating west, competing for available good land, soaked the earth in blood as they warred over the remaining good land driving everyone westward before them. Both of these scenarios of history are firmly in place. This foretold prophecy of the above scripture and the event presented by these researchers needs to be looked at in a new light. Chinese records of this time period document the mass evacuations and migrations of whole nations owing this event to the destruction

The Wilderness and Time

laid upon the land by dragons that scorched the land at their coming. It is well documented that comets were and are associated part and parcel with dragons of eastern lore. Chinese historical records of 540 A.D. say:

> "Dragons fought in the pond of the K'uho. They went westward... in the places they passed, all the trees were broken."

This is a perfect description of the Tunguska impact of 1908 A.D. the westward direction these (Dragons) took can be used to verify were these indeed comet fragment impacts, and are they related to the Taurid meteor stream, and the Tunguska impact.

Now, continuing onward in Revelation 8:8-12

> And the second angel sounded, and as it were a great mountain burning with fire was cast into the sea: "and the third part of the sea became blood; and the third part of the creatures which were in the sea, and had life, died; and the third part of the ships were destroyed. And the third angel sounded, and there fell a great star from Heaven, burning as it were a lamp, "and it fell upon the third part of the rivers, and upon the fountains of waters; "And the name of the star is called Wormwood: and the third part of the waters became wormwood; and many men died of the waters, because they were made bitter. And the fourth angel sounded, and the third part of the sun was smitten, and the third part of the moon, and the third part of the stars; so as the third part of them was darkened, and the day shone not for a third part of it, and the night likewise.

With the information of the Proto Krakatau eruption of 536 A.D. again we have a perfect description of an event that historically took place. This great burning mountain was cast into the sea as with the above scripture a great mountain burning with fire being cast into the sea. This is also in historical chronological order with the bombardment of the earth by fragments of a comet (hail mingled with fire and blood).

So, from the scientific community there are two opposing arguments to what caused the time we know of as the dark ages. Both present their cases accurately demonstrating the historical past and in doing so they unwittingly substantiate the prophetic. The darkness was the cumulative result of both. Even as it was seen by John in his vision, four hundred years earlier a vision that only could have come from the orchestrator of creation.

As we read on, it is prophesied the sun shone for only one third of the day. Documented witnesses of the time verify this was the case. All these events took place four hundred years after the Book of Revelation was written.

It is this priesthood, after the order of the way of Melchizedek that has foreseen the wobble of the earth's axis in the coming year of 2450 A.D. this was foretold that it would take place nearly seven thousand years before modern man came to this same conclusion. It is this priesthood, after the Order of the way of Melchizedek that prophesied the fact that Sirius would change from a red giant into a white dwarf and they did so nearly seven thousand years ago, five thousand years before the event took place. It is this priesthood that knows the Alpha and Omega; it is this priesthood that can only be entered into, by being a personal friend of the Living GOD. This is why John of Revelations knew of the coming Taurid meteor storm and the eruption of Proto Krakatau and the coming darkness. Followed by the bitter waters of Islam the star Wormwood, that rots from the inside with bitterness. For out of bitterness was it born and out of bitterness was it formed by the attempts of the Rabbinical Jews and merchants of Median in Arabia in their bid to regain Jerusalem from Byzantine occupations. They were subjugated by those they had given shelter to. This plan back fired with grave consequences for the Rabbinical Jew even to this day. In its beginnings all followers of Islam including Mohamed himself faced Jerusalem to pray not Mecca, and to this day bitterness is the defining spirit of the fountain of Islam. All this was foretold hundreds of years before these things happened by God Almighty through the

The Wilderness and Time

Apostle John. These are only the beginnings of woes for this planet. History and truth is a witness to these facts.

Now returning to the terminology of the "Dead in Christ" this refers exclusively to those people who have given up their lives for their testimony of Jesus Christ, before the antithesis of Christ the Beast. These are those people that have been martyred through the ages for expressing Jesus Christ's nature, good will to all men, with their faith and witness of his resurrection even to their own deaths. These will be and are blessed and holy forever, and they with those which have not taken the mark of the Beast in their hands (that is to say the works done by their hands) or in their foreheads (the leading thoughts guiding their minds) at the time of the return of Jesus Christ these shall reign with Christ a thousand years. But the rest of the dead lived not until the thousand years is completed.

Those people who call upon the Lord Jesus through the ages. Who lived in times of relative peace like many of our parents and grandparents and their parents before them, who lived their lives out not having to be killed for their witness of the risen Christ, lived not again until the completion of the thousand years at the time of Great Judgment. If their names are found in the Lambs book of Life, their lives will be spared. The first resurrection is for those that laid down their lives for Christ Jesus sake these are exempt from the Great Judgment. This is the testimony of John in Revelations' chapter 20 and his witness is true.

It is for us who now survive to keep his name, and live his expressed nature. This is done by his Living Spirit living in us. If you are his, this is your witness before all men. Whether secular or religious standing our ground having good-will to all mankind. With our hope in him that has been risen from the dead, the first fruit which we follow after. We will be raised with our lots some at the first resurrection and others at the Great Judgment when the books are opened. Scoffers will scoff, but how are you?

CHAPTER 10

The Voice of God
The Lord of Hosts

All the work of the Order after the way of Melchizedek points to all men to put on the robe God has made for them, so all can stand before God for themselves. The willfully ignorant will have no excuse.

All the work of The Order after the way of Melchizedek points to Jesus of Nazareth as the "One" born of a virgin; that brings us face to face with God through his life, and this is the very covering of our nakedness. Having been the voice of God made flesh, as the Order after the way of Melchizedek even now proclaims. He walked on earth and voluntarily hung his body on the tree. So that as many as will acknowledge the sacrifice of his life on that tree, and accept his body as their towel, as their robe; may clothe their nakedness with him. These that have erased the nakedness of their rebellion by the acknowledgement that this man Jesus of Nazareth was then and is now the Voice and consciousness of the Most High God and in Him and Him alone is our salvation found these will be saved.

It is by recognizing God in his body we clothe ourselves with him. By this we have the power to hear the Voice of God and walk with him even as Jesus is with him. This is the Gospel of Jesus Christ: that the enemies of your soul do not want you to know. For once someone puts him on in place of the fig leaves they now wear those that seek to dominate your soul will have no more power over you.

There is no need of you to join any denomination that claims to be the Church. God will guide you. You will appreciate other Christians that are Christians indeed. But beware of them that say you need to be under some kind of denominational authority, these do not believe the God they profess.

Jesus said:

> "When they say to you that I am in their inner chambers do not believe them." Matthew 24:26

You are responsible for your own salvation. It is written, work out your own salvation, there shall be no excuses. No one shall point the finger of blame for their own short comings at another, as Adam pointed the finger at Eve. The Spirit of Christ is responsible to teach you, and you are responsible to look to Him to learn of Him. He will do this, if the gift of faith that he has risen from the dead abides in you. If you then believe, that he is risen from the dead, your responsibility is to have no one before him or between Him and you. This is the first commandment.

It is by his Living Spirit He will speak to you and guide your heart, and you will know the truth and acknowledge His word if the word of truth abides in you. As a good father teaches his son his own virtues, that father is honored as he sees his son manifesting those virtues that he taught him, and that father is pleased with his creation in creation; so it is with your heavenly father.

From the moment his consciousness takes its place in your heart you will begin to see his creation for the first time as he begins revealing himself to you. Now you will know what it means to repent. Now you will begin to repent for the rest of your natural life. Now you will learn the true meaning of circumcision and be numbered with those that worship in his temple. The very same temple that John measured in the book of Revelation and that temple is His body and His body is the tree of life and the fruit of that tree is eternal life.

Some will commune with Jesus more than others and others

will hear Jesus more than others as well, even as your experience will vary from one another if you are indeed the good ground spoken of in the parable of the Sower. Mat 13:4-9

In this case be exceedingly happy and thankful to God, because this revealing of his voice as he puts his light on the deeds within your heart is his everlasting covenant and your eternal life. You will know your faults better than anyone else except for God himself. It is by this, his voice abiding in your heart; this is the only way you can change at his pace that He is working in you. Then the dark and not so pretty things in each and every one of us will be made to account for its action. By the same voice also He provides the remedy to us that will reconcile all the intents of our hearts with Him. Those that can see God in Jesus will also see man as the image of God.

> For God created man in his own image in the image of God created he him, male and female, created he them.

He that shows mercy to his fellow man shows mercy to his creator God, and God will do the same for that person. He that is angry with his fellow man without a just cause disrespects and dishonors God. Even as Jesus said:

> When the son of man shall come in his glory, and all the holy angels with him, then shall he sit upon the throne of his glory: And before him shall be gathered all the nations: And he shall separate them one from another as a shepherd divides the sheep from the goats: And he shall set the sheep on his right hand but the goats on his left. Then shall the king say unto those at his right hand. Come ye blessed of my father inherit the kingdom prepared for you from the foundations of the world: For I was hungry and you fed me I was thirsty and you gave me drink I was a stranger and you took me in. Naked and you clothed me: I was sick and you visited me. I was in

> prison and you came to me. Then shall the righteous answer him saying: Lord when did we see you hungry and feed you? or thirsty, and gave you a drink? When did we see you as a stranger and take you in? or naked and clothe you? or saw you sick or in prison and came to you: and then the king shall answer and say to them truly I say to you in as much as you have done it to one of these least of my brethren, you have done it to me. Then shall he say also to them at his left hand. Depart from me you are cursed into everlasting fire prepared for the devil and his angels. For I was hungry and you gave me nothing to eat. I was thirsty and you gave me nothing to drink. I was a stranger and you left me in the street. Naked and you clothed me not: Sick and in prison and you did not come to visit me.
>
> Then said they: When did we see you hungry or thirsty or a stranger or naked or sick or in prison and did not hold you? Then shall he answer to them saying: Truly I say to you inasmuch as you did not do it for the least of the one of these you did not do it for me.

In all respects a sin against your fellow man is a sin against God. On this principle, Jesus hung all the law and the prophets.

> Thou shalt love the LORD thy God with all your heart and with all your soul and with all your mind.
> This is the first and great commandment, and the second is like unto it. You shalt love thee neighbor as yourself. On these two commandments hang all the law and the prophets.

I am here to tell you, those who sacrifice their fellow human being, to uphold their religion and do so in preference to one another so that their dogmas of their religion become more important than the essence of God in their fellow human being, have totally lost their way. To revert to violence for the sake of doctrinal purity is simply one of the signs of the times of a lost world. Even as the apostles said would come, even as they warned of the wolves that would enter the church not sparing the flock; heaping disciples to themselves, these do not know the Living Jesus and worship their own religious creation, rather than God through the resurrected Christ living in their hearts.

These will be the ones that will say to the Lord... Lord, Lord have we not preached in your name? and in your name drove out (heretics) devils, and in your name done great and wonderful works. These will be the ones who the Lord will say to:

> Depart from me you worker of iniquity, I never knew you.

Neither have these people had faith in the Living Voice, in that they seek to be the Holy Spirit to you, with their own minds. In doing so they have done what is not their place to do. The revelation of truth is in the sole possession of the Holy Spirit. Those that usurp the Holy Spirit's place and seek to be the Holy Spirit for others, have climbed into the Father's bed and defiled it. They shall not prosper.

Those that can see man as the image of God and Jesus as the <u>expressed</u> image of God have the beginning of wisdom.

Everyone has Christ in them, this is the mystery hidden since before the foundation of the universe. The Gospel is the good news revealing this mystery, but the eyes of many have not yet been opened, the windows of heaven are revealed from within from the innermost recesses of the heart and then outward to the mind and soul.

Jesus Christ is the forerunner for all to come after him, the very course put in place, for us to run. He will honor everyone who follows after him on this course. No matter how many times they stumble, no matter what their errors are, it is in the getting up again and again that we learn to run the race, and the less we stumble the less others will stumble over us and in the end we are saved.

Those that hate Jesus Christ hate their own souls. Those that hate the Name of Jesus because of the offences they have received at the hands of those who sought only to overshadow and dominate you. By preaching his name at you yet never knowing him themselves. May the spirit of truth come to you and comfort you and lift you up and put your feet on his course again. Those that have done this to you it will be better that a mill stone is tied to their necks and they be cast into the depths of the sea. Jesus said:

> I desire mercy not sacrifice, all manner of sin and blaspheme will be forgiven, but blaspheme of the Holy Ghost shall never be forgiven.

So what is the voice of God and how can you know it is God? His voice his anointing in you will enable you to recognize when men quote the scriptures of their own accord. You will learn this by the inner dealing of his voice in your soul by putting his calling above all things, by abiding in that very calling that brought you to your salvation from the beginning. He will show you the word of God when it is spoken even when they are not quoting the scriptures and what is not the word of God even when they do quote the scriptures. He will teach all them that abide in him all things in their proper time at his pace, he is Lord and you are host. Abide in him and he will abide in you and teach you all you need to know. You will make your share of mistakes make no mistake about that, but if you abide in him your first calling even your presumptuous errors he will use as a tool to abide in his voice. Any teaching or any doctrine that does not encourage and bring you into a more intimate union with his Living being in a personal way is theology and a thief. The voice of God always increases your faith in Him that he is a Living God and is able to lead you. The voice of God proclaims what the angels heralded when Jesus was born and without exception!! And that is Glory to God in the highest, and on earth good will toward men. He searches the motives of what one hears in the heart, so that one learns the voice of God as one listens. The voice of God is the mind and nature of Jesus Christ, never forget that, he always speaks the truth. If what you follow does not come to pass it was not God and you have fallen down again, it is like being a newborn learning to walk if you believe that he is risen from the dead, you will get up again. Jesus said mine know my voice from others they turn way even within ourselves yet He is even more. There is no vision or revelation or dream from God that condones what is not of the nature of Jesus Christ. For in understanding and learning Him one comes to know his voice when he speaks from out of all the background noises of this life. His voice always brings the knowledge of the remedy; it always brings repentance, <u>yet never condemnation</u>. It is always a light shining on darkness. This always leads to independence from the words of man, yet He shows you the word of God in man. Not so others are to lead you, but rather it shows you your brothers and sisters in Christ. The Word always goes deep past the thoughts of the mind of ones own self. To the very quick of your being, it is a quickening and oneness in the mind of Jesus. He always reconciles the issue with God the Father's will even when this quickening is chastisement of our souls, the voice of God always bears witness to Jesus and never to itself. There is only a circumcision to life from death for death is passing by in our time of judgment even now; for as many as wrap themselves in him and have the courage to put him on the throne of their heart. They are the hosts and he is our Lord.

The Lord of Hosts first appears in the Bible as a title, in the book of 1st Samuel at around the time of King David, and is magnified in use by the King; and especially by the prophet Isaiah later on. But it is in the time of the exodus in Exodus 12:40-41 the children of Israel are first called a peculiar name; they are referred to as the Hosts of the Lord, four hundred years earlier than the time of Samuel and King David this reference the Hosts of the Lord, is the sum of what I am saying. This denotes the indwelling or that they are carrying the prophecy of the indwelling of God in their bodies. Like when someone has the flu, but in a positive way, he or she would be the host or hosts of that indwelling germ. Paul writes in Colossians 1:26-27

> Even the mystery which has been hidden from ages and from generations after generation, but now is made known to his people: To them God would reveal what is the riches and glory of this mystery

Among the Gentiles and that is Christ in you the hope of glory.

This is what was shown to Abraham; this is the sign of God's everlasting covenant with man. This sign or token of circumcision is the message we today who believe by the prompting of the Voice of God circumspecting and guiding our lives, by acknowledging those things in our lives that his Holy Spirit shows us as profitable and unprofitable for our souls. This can only be done by his Holy Spirit. When it is by the prompting of men it is always unprofitable, and leads people away from God and the development of the traditions of men. The message here is God is in you, and you must trust him. Ask him to guide you personally. He has said, "...if you being evil know how, to give good gifts to your children, how much more will your heavenly father give good gifts to those who ask him."

Those that hate your soul will always say "You can't rely on God alone to guide you. Let us help guide you or perhaps you will fall into a cult if you trust in God alone." They will say they have tried and true methods for you to learn about God, "Join us there is safety in numbers trust what we say". These will lead you only to themselves, and the cult they warned you of by instilling doubt and fear will be the cult they bring you into. Such people do so because in their hearts they do not believe that Jesus of Nazareth is raised from the dead, so <u>they can't hear God,</u> and if they can't hear God, they do not want you to hear God. Because what they truly want is power over you and power over your pocket book.

Trust God! If you ask him for an egg he will not give you a scorpion. Trust the voice that calls from within. Ask him to distinguish himself from yourself and reveal himself to you. Trust God! You believe he is risen from the dead...Then trust Him!

This is the meaning of faith, and his title Lord of Hosts. He will discern the intents of your heart for your good. It was by this Abraham was counted as righteous by his faith.

Absolutely, God will use some people to advise you, but it is by his inner voice dwelling in you bearing witness that he will ring the bell of truth within you to what any say. Follow no man no matter how pious or what credentials they possess, rather keep your heart open for the calling of God and try the spirits. If that person's word is from God he will rejoice in your growing independence as the word of God grows in you...

"He must increase and I must decrease"

These are the words of the mightiest Holy man ever born of man concerning his position with the Almighty and you.

Now concerning circumcision in the flesh if the intent is to honor the everlasting covenant promised to Abraham which is Jesus Christ in you. Then the Law of Moses has nothing to do with it. Even as Jesus has said: "Moses gave you circumcision not because it is from Moses but because it is of Abraham" circumcision preceded the Law of Moses. If the Apostle Paul was here today I would rebuke him for his stand on this issue. If his stand is as it is recorded in his letter to the Galatians he states, "If anyone is circumcised he is a debtor to the Law and is fallen from grace." This statement at its face value is a lie. If Paul was confronting the issue of bringing people under the Law of Moses that is different but as it is stated, I would prevail, justified by God, because circumcision is the proverb in the flesh of the prophecy of Jesus Christ. Moses and the Law has nothing to do with it. But, most likely Paul would be correcting me for presuming he was so closed minded. Or maybe he will thank me for clarifying this subject for him. For by this, those that did not know God, who have gained positions of authority in the Church, have used this quotation to drive the circumcised in the flesh out of the congregations.

For in knowing the significance of circumcision's true meaning it is no wonder Jacob cursed two of his sons Simon and Levi. For after receiving the unction of God (circumcision) Shechem and his father and all the men of their city were slaughtered by Simon and Levi who killed them without mercy. Those who Simon and Levi had enticed to join with them and become Hosts of the Lord even as they were by their recent circumcision. Levi and Simon raised their swords to the Hosts of the Lord and struck and killed the promised temples of God as if striking God himself. The curse of their father Jacob laid on them reads as:

> Simon and Levi are brothers, instruments of cruelty are in their nature. O my soul, come not into their secret. Unto their assemble mine honor be not united with them. For in their anger they killed a man in their self-will they broke down the wall. Cursed is their anger, for fierce was their wrath it was cruel I will divide them in Jacob and scatter them in Israel.

In having this great mystery revealed, that God though his Christ dwells in you even in the first person, only the unenlightened and self-willed can endorse violence towards one another. It is no marvel that the early church thought it unthinkable for Christians to go to war. They went so far as, not even raise a hand to their pagan persecutors for the very same reason.

As I have already stated, it was not until Constantine and those that were in league with him came into power and restructured the church into its present form did this ever take place. With the end result to present Jesus as a warrior God and the Lord of Hosts as a warrior God. Why? Because they never knew him in the first place; they believed the lies of men instead of the voice of the Living God in their hearts. The word of the Lord was and is to them

> precept upon precept upon precept: line upon line upon line upon line here a little there a little they are taken captive in a snare and are fallen back.
> Isaiah 28:13

> So is it spoken: "He that lead others into captivity will be taken into captivity he that kills with the sword must be killed with the sword. Here is the patience and the faith of the saints." Rev 13:10.

> Who so ever sheds man's blood, by man shall his blood be shed: for in the image of God made he man. Genesis 9:6

It is just this kind of blind people now in control who now wished to teach the world about God. During the Middle Ages, those who dared declare that God spoke to them were burned at the stake, as witches, by these same beasts. Or in the case of the Puritans of Massachusetts they took those who claimed that God spoke to them and cut off their ears. Then asked them again if they still heard God, if they answered yes: the Puritans would hang them. To these beasts God is a word on paper formed by precept after precept and no longer a Living person. They debate the meanings of a word and follow the letter but his voice is far from them. Their nature is self evident. Thank God the earth has opened her mouth swallowed the flood of persecution and now we have separation of church and state, for a little time longer any ways.

All that these beasts can do is tell you about their carnal opinion of God, for they do not know him as they themselves struggle with interpreting all the scriptures. When the scriptures, that is to say, what is on paper is asserted and or affirmed as the Word of God rather than the acknowledging the Voice of the Living God, then it has become the most subtle form of idolatry and idolatry is what it is.

There are not two words of God that is a lie. The idea that there are two words of God is how so many are lead astray and taken into captivity by those who want you to follow them and their interpretation of scripture rather than the Living God. A God they do not know whether it is Old Testament or New Testament or Koran. They will say with their carnal understanding "is it scriptural," "Is it scriptural" spoken by the carnal mind is the banner of the Antichrist from the beginning.

The Lord of Hosts has said:

"You search the scripture for in them you think you find life and they do testify to me and you will not come to me, that you may have life and have it more abundantly."

There is but one Word of God the Lord Jesus Christ! I much appreciate the Holy Scriptures, to me they have been a witness that the voice I follow and the foundation being laid in my life, is by God Almighty embodied in Jesus of Nazareth. But the name and title, the Word of God I will give to no book. It is God's title alone, and I sanctify this title to Him and Him alone. This doctrine of the written word of God was developed by the bishops that enabled Constantine the emperor of Rome to seize control of the church they were Antichrists

It began with the laity that formed a cult around the departed Apostle Paul even as Paul told them they would do. They congregated in Nic-op'-olis at the imperial palace in Rome. Titus 3:12-14 and Acts 20:29-30. This was the start of this authoritarian movement and is referenced too by the Lord Jesus Christ in the book of Revelations, in his letters to the seven Churches of Asia. They are known and identified as false Apostles and labeled as Nic-o-la'-tanes, Nic-o-media is Latin for Nic-o-oplis. This cult continued in Rome and eventually won the ear of the emperor Constantine some 265 years later. Their counterfeiting of the epistles of Paul was well known in the early Church and is the reason why the Apostle John by the authority of the Lord Jesus Christ put a curse on anyone that tampered with the book of Revelations Rev. 22:18-19. It was this book of Revelations that Roman Church tried so hard to exclude from the biblical canon but the Churches that survived in Asia were having none of it.

There is also a clear disconnect in spirit from the earliest writings of Paul and the later writings attributed to his name, only those with the anointing shall see the difference. Jesus said "My sheep know my voice."

I know God Almighty because he is revealing himself to me. Because of this I know the testimonies of the witnesses of God in the Scriptures are true. My faith is not based on a book, half of the epistles of Paul could be tampered with, and the works of men as inserted lies into the Scriptures and it would not affect me at all, it does not matter to me, I don't worship a book. But what God reveals to me I know is true therefore I can understand the Scriptures as God chooses to reveal them to me. This is the only foundation I should be building my house on, as I am conformed to the mind of Christ who is in me and is working in me as he is continuing to reveal himself to me.

Who canonized the Scriptures and why? The same people who

used to burn people at the stake for believing God spoke to them to what the Scriptures do say... You shall know them by their fruits...Give that a long thought. When King David took a census of Israel he did so at the bidding of Satan and his actions vexed all Israel and David repented before the Lord for the evil that he had done. To canonize the Scriptures is the same as taking a census of the Scriptures, that is to say, there is no more to come. But the last book, Revelation, says there is much more to come, and it will be revealed at the closing moments of time. Yet it is these same blind people who canonized the Scriptures who seek to rule over you. It is this lack of understanding and unbelief that God is in them and they are the image of God, which causes them to do this, and causes all the violence and evil in this world for their own gain.

Even to this day Jews and Muslims slaughter one another both carrying the unction of God in their flesh. This is to say, they are both of the circumcision, but the meaning of this is far from them both.

The Muslims follow Mohammed, a man who claimed to be a prophet, yet his message is, "God does not speak to anyone anymore, I was the last to hear God. I am the prophet, follow my teaching that I put on paper." What kind of father in heaven is this that he does not speak to his own children? This doctrine is nothing new. Islam is just another form of Judaism or another form of Catholicism mixed with Arab nationalizm. Mohammed knew as much of God as Constantine did. None of them honor Abraham in their deeds. Abraham knew the everlasting covenant, he walked with Him. He sat down and ate bread with Him. The everlasting covenant is in all who believe the Voice of the Living God is in them, these are those who will sit and take bread with him in this life and the life to come.

All peoples, works go before them and their rewards will follow after them even as Jesus said "...you shall know them by their fruits." That is to say by their works. This is why Jacob cursed Simon and Levi as he did, because they had despised the consciousness of the indwelling of the Lord of Hosts in those new initiates of the Hosts of the Lord. For this reason Jacob (Israel) said of his sons "You have made my name to stink in the land." In that they (Simon and Levi) honored not the covenant of the Lord of Hosts even as they insisted these others to be initiated to them, and their father Jacob (Israel) endorsed this as he granted his daughter to Shechem in marriage. Jacob (Israel) like his father the child of promise Isaac honored the sign of the everlasting covenant with their works of their faith the deeds of their lives. That is to say God dwells in the tabernacles of the bodies of mankind. The fruits, that is to say the deeds of Isaac show this as clear as crystal in Genesis 26:12-22:

> Now Isaac sowed in that land and reaped in the same year a hundredfold. For the lord had blessed him, and the man became rich, and continued to grow richer until he became very wealthy; for he had possessions of flocks and herds and a great household, so that the Philistines envied him. Now all the wells which his father's servants had dug in the days of Abraham, his father the Philistines stopped up by filling them in with earth. So Isaac departed from there and camped in the valley of Gerar, and settled there. Then Isaac dug again the wells of water which had been dug in the days of his father Abraham, for the Philistines had stopped them up after the death of Abraham; and he gave them the same names which his father had given to them. But when Isaac's servants dug in the valley and found there a well of flowing water, the herdsman of Gerar quarreled with the herdsman of Isaac, saying the water is ours! So Isaac named the well strife, because they contended with him. Then they dug another well, and they quarreled over it too, so he named it "oppositions accusation" So he moved away from there and dug another well, and they did not quarrel over it; so he named that well "The Way", for he said, "At last the Lord has made room for us, and we will be fruitful in the land".

All the deeds of Isaac can be surmised and all that he did, by the teaching of Jesus and his Sermon on the Mount which exemplifies Isaac's life to the Tau. Mat 5:38-48.

He that calls Abraham, and Isaac, and Jacob their father let them do and acknowledge the deeds of Abraham, Isaac and Jacob in their own works. Let them walk as their fathers walked, let their conscience be as their fathers consciousness. Let them follow who their fathers followed, even as their fathers Abraham, Isaac and Jacob follow him. Then are you the sons and daughters of Abraham.

If you do the deeds of Simon and Levi, then Simon and Levi are your fathers and Jacob has said of them (Simon and Levi are brothers: instruments of cruelty are their habitations. O my soul come not thou into their secret: **unto their assembly, mine honor be not united**:) Jacob Genesis 49:5-6.

The motives of your heart will truly determine who your father is. On this foundation we all build on our lives. Even as Jesus said (Mat 7:24-27).

The sum of living here on earth is cradled in Jesus' Sermon on the Mount and was exemplified by Abraham, Isaac and Jacob, like all of us imperfect people, but these followed after the consciousness of the Living God while they were here on earth.

These three, modern Judaism, Islam and Catholicism and all those denominations modeled after Catholicism that are her daughters, they are all one and the same. The only difference is national pride. All three of these horns will be plucked out by the root and what comes up in their place will go into damnation. See Revelations 17, 18 and Daniel 7:7-8, 20-22.

These do not enter the temple of the Most High God for themselves and seek to bar those that would. If any of them truly believed God was their Father they would not try to stop others. But all three of them say and do the same things "God doesn't speak anymore we have our laws and traditions to follow stay in our guidelines or you will be killed". Except for the fact that the earth has opened her mouth for the time being this is what they would do to you for bucking their systems. They say we have written down all you need to know about God there is no more revelation, trust us.

Well my enemies of my soul who seek to prevent the blossoming of faith, my Father loves me and I love him I love to hear Him even when he chastises my soul in it I know He loves me. What use does the child of God that hears and knows Him have to do with your traditions of a God whom you do not know? If he were your father you would be happy for them that he calls by name.

For what purpose is there to follow traditions about God and not God himself? I liken it to reading a book about going to a park with your father. Or going to the park with your father, but when he calls to you saying; "come let us go to the park". You avoid him saying; no thanks we will read all about it... and learn what we want to think it was like to be with you. This to your own shame: Yet these are the same that forbid their brothers and sisters that would go, to go saying to them stay with us you can read all about him, don't go. This to their condemnation; repent if you can.

Yes, our Father is coming and he is in an angry mood towards the wayward. No longer will he allow anyone to prevent my brothers and sisters that desire to see their father, to do so any more. Those who stand in their way he will sweep away. Like chaff, in the wind, they will be blown away.

Babylon the Great is fallen. Her world systems are corrupt. She seeks only profit and gain, she sells the goods even the goods made by the hands of slaves, for a profit. The whole earth and all them in it buy her merchandise to save only a dime. She has made merchandise of us all. We have turned a blind eye to those who are afflicted at her hand, simple to save a dollar on a new pair of shoes.

She looks to her multitude of religions and traditions and the diversity of her peoples and cultures in all the earth to justify herself to God. Then she consumes the flesh of the innocent, the unborn, to improve the quality of her own life. Babylon the Great Mother of Harlots is fallen, she is fallen. Come out of her my people says the Lord. Turn your backs to her whoredoms. Her sins have reached unto heaven. She cannot cease of her sin and seeks only to make a profit even with the instruments of war. She wipes her chin and says I have done nothing wrong. I am a Queen, I am no whore. I follow the Rule of Law established by my king who I service.

Babylon the Great, the abomination of the nations is fallen, she is fallen. She is profane, she is consumed with her own greed. She sells justice to the rich and all the strength of the poor is consumed trying to protect themselves. The help offered from her hand is feeble and treacherous. She peaks from under her blindfold and puts her hand out to the rich for payment for her justice.

Her own afflicted Johns and envious lovers are putting the flame to her even while they lay with her. Her Rule of Law will not save her, the strong arm of men will not save her. All nations are drunk with the "wine of wrath" of her fornication. A double for her even as it is written. The great and the small, all that are in the earth behold her burning and still they do not repent of their evil; all of them whose names are not written in the Lamb's book of life.

The great and mighty and the small of the earth behold her. The Lord will judge in righteousness, he will not be mocked. It is Jesus and Jesus alone who is able to say in righteousness, "He that is not with Me is against Me."

The Lord will not be mocked, justice is mine says God. Your mercy will be determined by your mercy. Not even a sparrow falls to the ground except by the will of God. God is only your Lord when you are his host otherwise he is your adversary.

I close this part of this book certifying with my life that these things I have written here are true. My intention is to acknowledge truth and pass it on to those that can recognize it no matter what background they come from. **"Peace"** He that has an ear let him hear.

PART II

CHAPTER 11

My Beginning

At this time I would like to share some of the events that have taken place in my life that have brought me to this endeavor of writing this book.

I grew up in southern New Hampshire, about fifty miles northwest of Boston Massachusetts. The second son of five brothers, our household was a turbulent one to say the least. My father was French Roman Catholic and my mother American Baptist. My father insisted we were to be raised as Catholics. When I didn't make my confirmation to the Roman Catholic Church, this did not help things between my father and I. They had always been bad since my birth, but this was like adding gasoline to a fire. I was not supposed to have been born in the first place.

My mother and father were having problems of their own at the same time. When my father stopped going to church a few years later, me not making my confirmation to the Catholic Church was no longer such a big deal. But it added enough chaos of its own at the time. Never the less, even though he was no longer attending mass, he always disapproved of my mother reading to my brothers and I from the King James Bible. So, our household was quite dysfunctional until my mother and father divorced. I was twelve years old when this happened. For me life got better, but my mother had to work two jobs to make ends meet. My older brother watched

The Way of Melchizedek

me and my younger brothers at night, until he was sixteen or seventeen. Then, this duty fell to me.

So I watched my three younger brothers until I was seventeen. Then it was my younger brother's turn to watch the two youngest.

Now feeling free, more like liberated, I wanted to make up for lost time and to catch up with my friends from school in the social circles. I was quickly introduced to marijuana and became a pot head. I couldn't wait for the school week to be over and the weekend parties to begin. This had become my life, all through the last two years of high school.

Then at one particular party, I met this girl, and we had fun, and we were having fun all the time! Within six months she was pregnant. She thought of an abortion. She was so afraid of what her father was going to say when he heard that she was pregnant with my baby. But I was able to convince her to marry me instead. She did, and my first son was born. So here I was, a high school drop out; really, we were only children ourselves with a newborn baby in our arms trying to make ends meet.

I was nineteen years old, and she was eighteen when she became pregnant. I worked part time as a grocery clerk in a supermarket stocking shelves. It didn't take long before I was selling small time amounts of marijuana to supplement my income. Even though I had gotten pay raises and a promotion in the supermarket, I was making three times the amount of money selling pot than I could in the supermarket. Within a year I was up to my neck in marijuana dealing. I can say by experience, the higher you climb that ladder for connections the lower you go, with a lower class of people to deal with at every rung up that ladder you take, some of them were from very wealthy families, but still low class indeed. Eventually, I had a run in with one particularly low class person. I went an eye for an eye with him. He stole from me so I stole from him. I soon found myself running for my life. To finally escape I had to leave the country. So I joined the U.S. Army and was on my way to West Germany.

It took me nearly six months to bring my wife and son to West Germany but I managed even on a private's E-1 pay. Also in hind sight, I look back at this time in my life, and remember the analogy

My Beginning

that someone had once told me. If you put a jack-ass in a crate and ship him halfway around the world, when you open that crate you still have the same old jack-ass as before, nothing has changed. The only difference is now the jack-ass is on the other side of the earth. Just making a change of locations is never the answer. Without a change from within the heart, you're just wasting your time.

So here I was in West Germany, at the rank of private E-1, the lowest rank in the military with my wife and son, again trying to make ends meet. So I started black marketing; first just cigarettes and liquor, but I found the big money was in stereo equipment and beef from the American P.X. and of course selling hashish. The same ladder was there to climb, if you're going to get the best connections, and with the same caliber of people to deal with as in the United States.

I was soon doing more than just making ends meet. When I lived in West Germany, I lived like a king. I drove a Mercedes, my company commander drove an Opel. I was a private he was a captain, I had made a lot of German friends and connections, to the point I didn't want to leave Germany, I lived in opulence. I threw champagne parties for my friends. The champagne I bought from German border guards. Where they got the champagne or how they got it I never asked. I just paid the fifty cents a bottle they wanted, and took all they could supply. I could buy anything I wanted whenever I wanted it. But my time to leave West Germany and return to the United States was approaching fast. I was trying to get what was called a European Out. This is when you get your military discharge while you are still in Europe instead of returning to the United States. I had German sponsors and work lined up. But I also had an old hashish possession conviction from my first weekend in Germany and that came to throw a monkey wrench into those plans. So the European Out idea wasn't going to happen for me.

My next plan was to return to the U.S.A. and finish my time in the army and then return to West Germany as a civilian, and continue living the life I was leading.

Nine months after my wife had arrived in West Germany; my second son was born in Heidelberg. I wasn't at home much for him or his older brother or their mother. I was "doing my thing." As the

The Way of Melchizedek

time approached for my departure from Germany, some of my American friends, other U.S. soldiers, went out joy riding in the wine district around the city of Landau, not far from our duty station. It was a sunny Sunday afternoon. We drove around and drank wine and smoked hash for a couple of hours. We made a piss stop in front of a post office in a tiny village. The name of the village I can't remember. But after coming out from the back of the post office, I stopped to look at a wanted poster in the window. To see it surprised me, I had thought they only put up wanted posters in U.S. post offices. So, seeing this poster really surprised me. So I went to take a closer look. When I recognized the face on the poster I was stunned. It was a hashish connection I knew from Stuttgart. His name was Peter Willi Stoll. But I knew him only as Peter. The poster said he was wanted for the kidnapping and murder of the Vice President of West Germany. I was stunned! Just then I felt a presence and heard a voice in my heart. It said to me "Tom, Tom, where are you going? You know you're not living your life the right way." I tried to ignore the voice as I had in the past. It wasn't the first time I had felt its presence, or better put, its awareness. I had struggled with it in my heart before. Then I called my friends over to the window and pointed out to them it was Peter from Stuttgart. We were all amazed at what we saw and read. Shocked is more like the right word.

After getting over the initial shock we got back into the car. I said, wow! The guy in the front passenger seat said, "Where to now?" Then one of the guys in the back seat said "to hell if we don't change our ways." Everybody laughed. I went along with it, but I could only half-heartedly laugh at best. As I drove and entertained my passengers, I was thinking of that awareness and that voice in my heart. I knew it wasn't my own. In hind sight I wonder if the guy in the back seat was hearing the same voice. Maybe he didn't really laugh either.

In the following weeks partying was starting to lose its luster to me. But I continued on, by now I was an addict. And I can say that anyone who says that you can't get addicted to hashish or marijuana, well, I can tell them they're full of shit. I'm not trying to make a bad pun, but I'm aware of it.

My Beginning

I was smoking five to ten grams of hashish a day. Without it I didn't have my bodily functions. I couldn't keep down my food without it. I couldn't use the bathroom without it. I just wasn't having fun anymore.

I started reading a Bible my father had given me. I think it was a wedding present, but I'm not sure. I do remember how upset my mother was when he gave it to me. Mainly because of the way he had treated me my whole life. She thought it was insincerely given. They had been talking on the telephone when my mother told my father she was going to buy a Bible as a present for me. At hearing this my father went out quickly and bought a Catholic version and gave it to me before our wedding. That was how I even had a Bible in my house in the first place.

I think it was the very first time I opened it. That day when I came back from that joy ride in Landau, or shortly thereafter. As the weeks passed I had read most of Genesis, the first book of the Old Testament, excluding the long genealogies. My reading wasn't very good, that's why it took so long. Then I started reading the Gospel of St. Matthew, the first book of the New Testament. I remember reading that first night in the New Testament the Sermon on the Mount as it is called. As I read it, it was telling me the things I believed in my heart, but yet they were things I never had known or was never told. When I had finished reading Jesus' words of the Sermon on the Mount, the only thing I could say to myself was that this man has his shit together!

In the meantime, maybe that next morning, Peter Willi Stoll was gunned down in the city of Hamburg by the German police. When I heard, I thought of Peter and said to myself what a waste.

I began thinking of what I had put my wife through these last four years. Really, from the day I had met her. I told her I had wronged her in the strongest of words. I told her I would understand if she didn't want to have anything to do with me anymore. I told her, "I was no good, my father had been right from the beginning." I offered her everything we had to take with her if she wanted out. Then I packed my army gear and left on field maneuvers in the north near Breamerhaven for sixty days. When I walked out of my house that day, I felt about as tall as an ant. Oh how I had screwed up my life, I thought. She will be gone for sure when I get back, I thought. But I was hoping without much hope she would still be there.

When I returned from what was my last military maneuver in Germany, I was really depressed. When I put my key in my apartment door I thought, she's gone for sure. I turned the key and threw the door open, depressed and angered at myself for my own stupidness I was expecting to find an empty apartment, but I was greeted by the biggest "Hi you're home!" This I will remember for the rest of my life. Even writing about it some twenty years later makes me have to fight back the tears just thinking about it.

When I saw her I asked in disbelief "What are you doing here, why didn't you leave!" She told me she had become a Christian...I didn't care, I was just happy to see her!

But I still had all my problems. I was still an addict, my time in Germany was down to weeks. I had people that owed me thousands of dollars that I needed to collect from. I did what I had to do for someone in that business if you're going to be successful in that business. Now, two days shy from leaving Germany business was finished. I thought to myself, you did it, they didn't get me I won! But in my heart of hearts I knew I was lying to myself and it was only a matter of time. I saw Peter Willi Stoll's future waiting for me also.

I had felt as tall as an ant when I had left on maneuvers some two and a half months before. Now I felt so small, and so low, I could have walked under that ant and not even touched the top of my head on the bottom of that ant's belly. I had no future, I had done whatever it took to succeed but my life was nothing but shit.

At that moment all alone in my living room while I was still looking at stacks upon stacks of stacks of twenty dollar bills, I bowed my head and started to ask God for forgiveness.

But before I could even utter a single word, I heard that voice in my heart and felt that presence and that awareness that I spoke of at that post office, and I knew I was not alone in that room. The voice said to me in a firm, almost loud and stern manner, "You are not worthy to pray to me, sitting up in that chair." I paused for a moment confused and alarmed and I can recall how I had never heard such quietness or felt such stillness in all my life. It was like

My Beginning

booming thunder. It was the sound of my own heart beating! Then, shaken through and through, I got down on my knees and started to pray again. Then I heard the voice again, and he said, "You are not worthy to pray to me on your knees!" A fear fell over me like nothing I had ever experienced in my entire life, even to this day.

I said within myself at that moment "I'm going to die." I was aware I was in the presence of holiness. I fell immediately face down on the floor with my hands and arms out straight, then it was as if a dam had broken inside of me and all the deeds of my life were pouring out onto the floor in front of me. I asked God to forgive me as each deed came out. This went on for what seemed to be hours, as intense a pace as anyone reading can possibly comprehend. I had my first real confession! When it was over I felt as if I had drained my soul and I got up off the floor and sat down on the chair at the table where all this had started some hours earlier. Then I asked myself "What's happening to me," and before I could finish asking myself that question...I heard that still small voice in my heart say in the calmest and most serene voice say, "You have done that (speaking of my confession) now will you follow me." Again, the silence was deafening. Then I had my first vision. It was of a paratrooper preparing to jump out of a plane for his first time. I paused and swallowed my heart and said while I stood in the doorway of the airplane over the roar of the wind, "I will follow you but I can't do it without making mistakes," and the voice said... "that is all that I ask." And I jumped.

Then I had another vision. A heart appeared over my head and split open as if a lightening bolt had passed between the two halves and water poured out from the heart and poured into my heart and soul. It was living water, the love of God. And it filled me that night. Then an awareness came over me and I began to cry and the crying turned into mourning. I was crying my heart out, but I wasn't crying for me. I was crying for everyone in the world that had not experienced the love and forgiveness of God through Jesus Christ. This is why I cried and when all these things were finished, I was at peace with myself for the first time in my life and I went to sleep, I was very tired. When I awoke the next morning, I had some paperwork that needed signing at headquarters approximately 12 kms

The Way of Melchizedek

from where I lived. I was leaving Germany the next day but I noticed a peace inside me that I never felt before. So I decided to walk the 12 kms to headquarters. But the first car going by stopped and offered me a ride. I wasn't hitch-hiking but took his offer anyway. We didn't talk much, I was just enjoying the countryside as we rode, it was like I was looking at it for the first time in my life, even though I had seen it all a thousand times before. Then to my surprise, he turned left without instruction from me, and drove to the army post I was stationed at. There were five different army posts in the general vicinity and he dropped me off at the front gate. How he knew which was my duty station, I am not sure. He shook my hand and said to me in the German language, "Until we meet again," and drove away. I took care of the paperwork I had at headquarters then visited with some of my friends for a while. I told them what had happened to me the night before. The first thing one of them said to me was, "Were you tripping on acid or something?" I told them, "No, *this is what happened!*" Some of them became enraged with me and left the room. Those that stayed, I finished telling them what had happened to me. Then I said my good byes, shook hands and parted their company.

So I began my 12 km walk home to Lincolnheim. While I was walking I thought for a while and asked myself, "Why did some of my friends get so angry at what I told them?" I couldn't understand their reaction to what I had said.

As I approached the village of Eggenstein, I was simply worshipping God, thanking him for what he had done in me. While I worshipped him while I was walking, above the village I saw in a vision a light brighter than the sun. It was as if it was at a great distance away, coming toward me, closer and closer, until everything was enveloped by the light, and all there was, was the light.

I looked into the center of the light and saw a throne and the image of a man sitting on the throne. The man and the throne were both clear, transparent, like crystal and I saw the man clear as crystal, moving about as he sat on the throne. The light shined from out of the midst of the center of the man that was on the throne and the light was alive, it was living in itself. It shined through the man on the throne and there was no end to its depth. There was water like a

My Beginning

river flowing from his feet. I recognized the water, I could feel it! It was the same water from the night before that flowed into my heart from his heart. I began to worship the light and the man on the throne. I knew in my heart, to worship one was to worship the other, and I could only worship the light by worshipping the man from which the light came. For the two were inseparable they were one.

Then a man in a white robe, very tall and strong, was standing next to me. Then he took me to a place half way from the village down below, and the throne and the man who sat on the throne above. The living water that flowed like a river from the feet of him that sat on the throne, which was clear as crystal, formed a sea around the base of the throne in mid heaven. The man sitting on the throne was exceedingly tall, that no measurement feels right to put to him. Lower at earth's level was a multitude of people, I can think of no better way to put it.

Then the man in the white robe said only: "Watch." I saw one step out from the multitude and he was judged. Then he became a lightening bolt and flashed up to the sea of living water and flashed again and there was a star shining on the sea of living water. Then the next one stepped out from the multitude of people and became a lightening bolt speeding up to the sea of living water then he also became a star. I watched this happen over and over and over again with amazement and fear until the sea was completely filled with stars, so the man sitting on the throne clear as crystal and the brilliant light that shined outward forever rested on a sea of stars. It was the most beautiful and awesome sight I have ever seen!

Then the vision changed and it was I who was stepping out from the multitude of people, and I fell to my knees and bowed my head as low as I could make it go. Then my life was laid out before me to see. I was aware it was my life as a Christian, I was afraid and sorrow filled my heart. I looked up and saw only the engulfing light. Then the man on the throne said "Go your own way." Distress and anxiety gripped me for a moment, as I took to heart what was said to me. Then I thrust forward toward the man as clear as crystal, sitting on the throne, with tears pouring from my eyes and I wailed out with all my heart and all my strength and said, "My way is your way; and your way is Yahweh!"

When these words poured out from me I was startled I had been worshipping Jehovah and Jesus as one, I had never heard of Yahweh! But this was My GOD! Weeks later I discovered that Yahweh is the Hebrew word that we English speaking people call Jehovah.

Then I saw my star shining on the sea of living water. I also saw paradise on earth and the Throne room and Temple of God and he said to me, "You will be a living pillar in my temple," and he also said, "You will sit with me on my Throne." But I saw myself with my arms and legs wrapped around his big toe as I clung to his big toe with the biggest smile of my life as I was looking back at myself from within the vision!

Then the vision began to subside and I found myself on the other side of the village of Eggenstein worshipping My GOD with all my heart soul and mind. Then the water that had filled me the night before that also flowed from the throne began flowing out of me as I worshipped and I started worshipping in another language. So I covered my mouth because I did not know what I was saying, and started worshipping in English again. Within a few minutes I was speaking in another language again that I did not know. I had a new awareness. I was clean. More white than new snow and I covered my mouth again. By now the vision had passed but the new awareness was vivid and he said to me, "all your sins are forgiven, even all the sins you will every commit as well." In my heart I didn't think at that point I would ever sin again. In my heart I didn't want to sin ever again, but I have, and I still do, but in my soul I still do not want to sin. When I got home I knew I would never be the same again and I worshipped My GOD and thanked him for that.

CHAPTER 12

Back in the USA

In the morning I departed Germany for the USA on January 29, 1979. My next place of military duty and where I received my discharge was at Ft. Benning, Georgia, on the Chattahoochee River. Just the other side of the river was Phoenix city, Alabama. I rented an apartment there it was about 15 minutes away from my duty station at Ft. Benning. I was still getting sick if I didn't have marijuana. I had tried to quit twice already since leaving Germany. Both times I lasted only a couple of days. I had been praying about it and asked for help. I was still processing in when I was at one of the many departments on post that was part of the whole in-processing thing when I received a vision. It was of a woman ice skater making figure eights on the ice. But every time she made a mistake, she left a mark on the ice. At times she fell and gouged the ice making a mess of all the patterns that she was endeavoring to complete. But her determination pushed her on to finish and even though the ice was a mess and her failures were obvious, she strived for perfection as if she had never put a mark on the ice at all and while she continued skating, the sun rose high in the sky and melted the ice, and all the woman's mistakes disappeared. Now she was happily swimming in a lake and the water was eternal life.

About a week after I had this vision, a long weekend was coming up. It was during the February holidays and my wife and I

The Way of Melchizedek

decided to visit my father in Florida. I wished to salvage some kind of relationship with him, and I was trying to quit marijuana again at the same time. We drove to Florida to his house in Coco Beach. He hadn't seen me for four years, maybe since just after my wedding. When he saw me the first thing he said was "Are you still on the shit?"(meaning the marijuana) Well, I settled my wife and children in for the night and we had an awkward dinner with my father and his new wife, then I left by myself and headed for the beach to buy some weed. My father's greeting and attitude drained the will to fight completely out of me, or maybe I just used it as an excuse God only knows. I found some marijuana really quickly, and it was potent and cheap. So I took all the money I had, except for enough money to get us back to Alabama and enough for one day at Disney World, and spent the rest on dope. I went back to my father's place and laid on his hammock in his back yard and got stoned. As high as I was I felt terrible. I had ruined my family's weekend, just so I could stay high inexpensively for a couple of weeks at best.

When the weeks went by and I was down to my last joint, my wife asked me to go to the store for some milk. I got in my van and took my last joint with me and headed down the road, it was about two miles to the store. I lit the joint as soon as I left the apartment complex. I drew in my first inhale off the joint and I lifted the joint up to heaven and exhaled and said, "God deliver me from my affliction," and he spoke to me and said, "Throw it out the window," so I did. Then shortly got to the store and bought the milk and went home.

When I got home I put the milk in the refrigerator and sat on the couch. I was thinking the monkey is going to be on my back in the morning. Then the Lord spoke and said, "Throw out all your drug paraphernalia, all your literature that promotes drug use, and all your music that glorifies drug use," so I did. My wife must have thought I was going crazy at first, but happy I'm sure to see what I was doing as I flung album after album out the sliding doors into the woods behind our apartment. When that was finished I turned on the television and the first thing I heard was a television evangelist named Pat Robertson, and he said "The Lord Jesus has just delivered a man of marijuana addiction." Then I thanked God and went for a walk. May God bless Pat Robertson in all his doings and bring him back to his Living Word.

The next day when morning came, I awoke with no monkeys on my back and haven't had any since. Thank you Jesus.

I finished my time with the US Army in October, '79 and hoped things had cooled down in my home town enough that we could move back and live safely. So, we went back to New Hampshire, and lived a quiet life free from drugs and just tried to be the best father and husband I could be. Life was normal and relatively peaceful except for a reoccurring eye infection that my oldest son was always struggling with. I think it was a severe form of conjunctivitis. But we got medicine for him that helped keep it in check somewhat. We always prayed for a healing and hoped every morning it would be gone.

Some time went by and I had started studying the Bible and attended various Bible study groups. I thought some were good and others I thought just distracted me from the Voice of God with all their religiosity.

One evening while I was studying at my desk I was rereading Genesis Chapter 17 when God makes his covenant with Abraham, and I started laughing and said, "Lord Jesus, why circumcise the foreskin of a man's penis as the everlasting covenant!" Immediately he answered me as if he was waiting for me to ask this question. He said "It is the sign! of the everlasting covenant." At the same time I had a vision where I saw myself standing in darkness and the skin of my body was peeled down from my head to my feet and what was revealed was not my skeleton and muscle tissue, but a light brighter than the sun and the image of a man clear as crystal, and the light shone threw him, He was my GOD. I was humbled and have never laughed at any of the things in the Bible that I don't understand. But this was made clear as crystal to me.

I had went to so many different church groups, many would not even allow me to share my testimony of Jesus Christ. Then, I started attending a small fringe group that accepted me, and allowed people to share what their experiences were in the Lord, with the group. At the same time my oldest son's chronic eye infection had returned, and it was worse than ever. We took him to a doctor. The doctor told us if it didn't clear up soon it would lead to blindness later. We tried every medicine the doctors would prescribe and every reoccurrence was worst than the last.

One of the leading members of the fringe group I was fellowshipping with was traveling through the congregations in North America before leaving for Burma to do missionary work. He was speaking in Salem, NH, just two towns to the east of my home. I had prayed time and time again for my son's eye problem, but with no relief. Then, while I was at work, the Lord spoke and told me to bring my son to this man who was speaking in Salem, and have him pray for the healing of my son's eyes. He was speaking that night, it was a Wednesday night.

We went to the meeting and to my surprise, the service was in Spanish with an English translator, and most of the congregation was Latino. When the service was concluded I introduced myself to this man and told him the Lord had instructed me to bring my son to him to have him pray for my son's eyes. He told me he was a teacher, not a healer, and started to turn away. I put my hand on his shoulder and said, "I am just like you, trying to do my best to do what God wants me to do, and he told me to ask you to pray for my son. He looked down at my son and I could see the concern in his face. Then he put his hands on my son's head and prayed for his health. With that he took his handkerchief and wiped away the green slime that was oozing from my son's eyes. My son was five or six years old at the time, and remembers this to this day like I do, like it was just yesterday. My son will be twenty-six in January, and never once has this infection returned. Lindin Eldredge went off to Burma and I never saw him again. I thank God every time this event comes to my memory, and send my heartfelt best wishes to Linden Eldredge wherever the Lord takes him.

Life continued on uneventful for the most part, for the next two years. But I felt I was slipping away from my place with My GOD. I prayed harder and I read my Bible and studied it with all the more fervor and zeal but it wasn't preventing the slide from my place with God I wasn't hearing him like I had I looked to circumspect my life with the Bible in hopes to return to the place I had with God again, but I was only becoming more religious.

Then I had a dream that was more than a dream. The dream was as follows:

Two friends and I had finally found a large old farm where we could start a Christian community modeled after the church in the early part of the Book of Acts. When we took possession of the property, we started cleaning out one of the attics over the garage and found that another Christian group had come to this place to do the same thing and some of them still lived in the area on the farm. So we continued cleaning in the attic and I found an old rusty sword, but it had a beautiful jewel in its handle. I admired its workmanship and showed it to my friends. They both acknowledged it was a nice find. Instead of throwing it away, I kept it for myself and sheathed it in my belt. Then, one of my friends found an old newspaper, and in it was an announcement that a coven of witches were having their annual event at the cinema in town. They were commemorating their victories over all the Christian groups that had come to town. We were infuriated to read of this blaspheme, and noticed the date of their annual event was that very coming night. We took the newspaper to the people that had still lived on the farm from the last Christian group, and asked them what they knew of this coven of witches and this annual event to be held at the cinema. They were frightened and looked around then whispered in hushed voices warning us not to go near them and be careful what we say for fear we may be found out. We were outraged at this and were determined to confront them at the cinema that night!

That evening we went to the cinema. The witches were showing movies of all the Christian groups they had defeated, and how they had imprisoned, and caged, the different leaders of the Christian groups that had come to the farm for centuries. They exalted Lucifer as the Most High. At that we rose from our seats and proclaimed Jesus Christ was the Son of GOD the Most High God, ruler of heaven and earth.

The dream changed and we were now outside the cinema and continued our proclamation that Jesus was Son of the Most High GOD. The confrontation continued and a large crowd was gathering against us. It was night now and the crowd grew larger and angrier and started moving toward us. We moved back along the road, then ducked into some bushes along the side of the road. The witches began beating the bushes looking for us. Then one came upon me as I hid in the bushes and then I took the sword that I had found and thrust it through his solar plexus and the witch let out a shriek and ran down the embankment. I felt bad for stabbing him and went off after him to apologize and tell him how much he had been deceived. I chased him on and on over hills and through fields, but could not catch up with him.

I was now standing in the middle of an orchard, all alone. It was dark and eerie, there were no fruit or leaves on the trees. I was separated from my friends. Everything had gone wrong, we were losing, and the darkness was oppressive from all sides. Then I heard the Voice of God out of the darkness, and he said to me, "Throw away that rusty sword and take my Living Word." It wasn't easy to do, I trusted the sword. But, by faith, I listened and threw down the sword and took his Living Word.

At that moment, I could see the first signs of the sunrise on the horizon, and I began to walk toward it over hills and fields. Then I could see a farm house off in the distance on a hill, and the Living Word guided me to it. When I came to it I entered. I could see profanity and blaspheme written on the walls, but it wasn't profane the way one would normally think of profane, what was profane was they were all names of (religious groups) denominations claiming to be God's Church but were not and that was their blaspheme. It was the house of the witches, but none came out to confront me. I found my way to the cellar where there were cages filled with Christians, including the leaders of the different Christian groups that had lived on the farm before us, that had been imprisoned in the past, they looked old and hungry and sad with long white beards and there were my two friends also who went to the cinema with me to confront the witches. I opened the doors of the cages and set them free. Now the dream changed again.

I was standing on a hill with my two friends overlooking a long lake. At one end of the lake nearest us, a race was about to start, but the boats in the race weren't right. They all looked like they were rides from an amusement park, like in a merry-go-round or carousel. The first boat was a white swan and the second was like a Herbie the Love Bug, from the Walt Disney movies. The third was a silver gravy bowl, and the fourth was a black duck, like a mud hen. As they lined up for the race they floundered in the lake water like a child's toys in a bath tub. Then the starter's gun went off and at the same time we started walking with giant steps toward the lakeshore. When we reached the lakeshore we kept on walking. We were in the race; we were walking on the water. Then we were running across the water. Then we were flying across the water like cruise missiles heading for a target. We flew just above the water for the length of the long lake. At the far end of the lake there was an isthmus of land and then another lake running north to south, opposite of the lake we were flying over that ran west to east. When we had reached the eastern shore, we came upon a house a little way from the lakeshore. The house was inhabited by the witches. They watched us curiously from the second floor windows as we approached the house. Then we raised all our hands toward heaven and acknowledged the Most High God who lives forever and ever then we laid hold the sills of the house and lifted the house off of one side of its foundation and slammed it to the ground then again three times. The witches were falling out of the windows in shock. Then we turned the house over onto its roof and walked through its entrance like men of war. Inside we found three young girls huddled in a corner, trying to blow small goat horns to call the devil for help. We took the horns from them and crushed them with our hands. At that instant all their fear of us left them and we took them by the hand and walked out of the overturned house.

When we got outside it was like morning on a fresh spring day. All the neighbors in the area came out from hiding and asked us what had happened, and we told them the Kingdom of God has come! And I awoke!

The four boats that looked like rides on a merry-go-round that floundered in the lake like toys in a bath tub are the four pet doctrines of the people who think that these are the teachings of the God to his church. The first the white swan is the teaching and attitude held by those that see themselves above others because they follow the doctrine of being born again. The second Herbie the Love

Bug is the doctrine and teaching of love as a goody goody thing in itself; but with all its attempts it only produces a superficial kind of love. They attempt and teach this rather than communing with the Living God, where real love comes naturally. The third the silver gravy bowel, is the prosperity doctrine that has made only those who teach it wealthy at the expense of the desperate; teaching gain is Godliness. The fourth the black duck I don't know I am not quiet sure but I think it is like the black sheep idea. All of them are doctrines focused on things and outcomes instead of faith in the hearing of the Voice of God and that is why they flounder in the lake.

The Bible is not the word of God. Jesus is the word of God there is no other, the many witnesses to whom the word of God came by, with their testimony is just that; their testimonies of their witness of the word of God, written down on paper. That is "all" the Bible is, a convenient census of many testimonies of those that heard the Word of God. To look at the Bible in any other way is Idolatry.

Unless God is revealing himself to you, in the first person, of his son, Jesus of Nazareth, you do not know him, and you will not be able to face him. I know him as Yahweh, the Father, expressed to me as Jesus by Jesus. The sin of man causes him to hide himself from the presence of God among the trees because of his rebellion. Such persons have made themselves judges of the universe in the place of God. Yet man, for the most part, desperately tries to reconcile his judgment with God's but this is impossible. This is why there are so many thousands of thousands of interpretations of the scriptures and none are acceptable to God. Only the word of GOD the revealing voice of Jesus, as it is revealed to you is true. Yet millions and millions have their confidence in their own natural understanding of a book, or they follow what someone else tells them this book should mean. All this is a form of idolatry. It is old covenant. Believe what Jesus did for all mankind. All mankind!! And God will lead you himself. This is what this dream means to me.

This dream has been brought back to me by the Holy Spirit, over and over, as if it was both personally prophetic as to the events in my own life, as they are still unfolding before me as many other dreams as well. Also, as the churches eventual and final victory over the usurpers of God's inheritance among God's people. To me this dream speaks; it is only by living the Living Word and by walking with the Living God, and walking only when the Living God says walk that we as a people will experience his victory. Even as Jesus said to Peter:

> Blessed are you Simon for flesh and blood as not shown this to you but my Father in heaven and upon this rock I will build my church and the gates of hell will not prevail against it:

In all that I have said so far in this book and all that is said here after is this: Don't believe me don't take my word for anything, take God's Voice to your heart and live by that, the best you can, and when you come up short ask him for more. I do not want anyone following me or looking for me to tell them what God is saying to them that is the Holy Ghost's place. All I am saying is open your eyes and ears, and ask God in heaven to guide you the way he guided Abraham and King David, Isaiah and Daniel. These men walked by their revelation with the Living God as he dealt directly with them the same as with Peter, Paul and John and Ananias of Damascus. All these men had nothing to verify that it was God speaking to them and acted by faith in the voice at the moment they heard it. There were no scriptures for Ananias of Damascus to refer to when he heard a voice say, "Go to the street that is called straight." The only thing he could do was hope and wait until the fruits of his deed became manifest by the life and ministry of Saul of Tarsus.

This is what I feel Jesus was and is saying to me, he even said in the scriptures: to those that were obsessed with the scriptures:

> "You search the scriptures for in them you think you have eternal life and they are they which testify of me. But you will not come to me that you might have life, and have it more abundantly".

The Bible is a book of many books of many witnesses of God. No one should have their faith in a book. All should have their faith

The Way of Melchizedek

in the living God so that they are Yahweh's (Jehovah's) witness here on earth. I have had many who say they are Jehovah's Witnesses come to my home in an attempt to recruit me to their organization. Then I will ask them, "You are Jehovah's witness?" They always say yes. Then I will ask them, "Have you seen Jehovah yourself, face to face in the first person or in a vision?" They always say no then say... "but the Bible says...," or they will say, "Yes, through the Bible." Then I will ask them "Have you heard his voice? has he personally given you a message other than how you interpret the Bible? Has he spoken out from the darkness from out of obscurity and called you by name and spoken with you?" and they will always say "No", then they will say "but the Bible says..." Then I will stop them and tell them, "If you read in the newspaper of a train wreck in India, or a bombing in Ireland, does that make you a witness of that train wreck or bombing, just because you read about it?" If they are honest and sincere people, they will always say "No." Then I will ask them if your friend that you brought here with you, tells you that he saw someone from your church steal the mail from his neighbor's mail box, does this make you a witness of the theft also, because he told you so? If they are sincere and honest, they will say no. Then I will inform them by their own mouths they are not Jehovah's witness.

Then I will tell them, "But I am a witness of Jehovah. I have seen him. What do you want to tell me, of someone you have not seen or have not spoken to you?" Some run for the door, others want to hear more because they want the same thing for themselves. If they stay, the first thing I tell them is "I am a sinner."

But I am here to tell you what goes for Jehovah's witnesses goes for all that witness for Jesus in the same way. If you believe the old spiritual hymn: Jesus loves me yes I know for the Bible tells me so and that is the basis of your faith, then you are practicing a form of idolatry. Jesus loves me, yes I know for **he** the Living God, MY GOD the Resurrected Jesus, has shown me **he** is so. I acknowledge his witnesses in the book called the Bible because MY GOD has showed me their testimonies of him is true.

CHAPTER 13

Stepping Out

At about this time my third son was born and I also began having reoccurring dreams of going to China. Even in these reoccurring dreams I saw that I would fail at my task of following the voice of God and I did just that. I was given very specific instructions from the Lord in a dream to fly on Canadian Airlines from Vancouver, B.C.

In this dream I was told the airline, the day and the flight time. But, when I got to Vancouver, there was a Japan Airline's plane leaving several hours earlier and it was cheaper. This was the beginning of some very hard lessons for me to learn. Hopefully I have learned them by now. God knows.

I took the Japan Airlines plane instead of the one God had told me to take. About two hours from Hong Kong I fell asleep and dreamed. In the dream I was told not to go through customs and immigration, but to wait and a Chinese man would meet me and help me through immigration, and provide me with a place to stay. When the plane landed I got off and waited, and when the crowd had thinned to nothing, I doubted the instruction I had received from the Lord. Then I attempted to go through immigration on my own. They inspected my papers and found a form unsigned that had needed a signature from the English Consulate in Boston. I needed this signature to go to the University of Hong Kong. This was also my idea, this school thing. Without this signature from Boston, I could only stay for one week unless I found a sponsor. The next thing I know I am standing on the streets of Kowloon with one week to find a sponsor, but I did know of a group of Chinese Christians pioneered by an evangelist called Watchman Nee. I also knew his work had been splintered by opposing leaders in the church vying for control after his death at the hands of the communists on the mainland.

So, which group was the right group? Finally I decided any group was better than what was happening now! I searched that whole week in vain and was soon on a plane for San Francisco. When I arrived in San Francisco I called an old army friend whose family's phone number I had kept all these years in my wallet. I stayed with him and his wife and daughter for two days. Then with maybe fifteen dollars in my pocket, I started hitchhiking back to New Hampshire.

By the time I reached Boise, Idaho, I was down to my last quarter, but I had friends in Boise from the same Christian group I attended in New Hampshire.

They had moved to Idaho seven or eight months earlier, so I looked in a phone book at a truck stop and found their name. Then I took out my last quarter my last quarter! and dialed the number, hoping and praying they would be home. Cheryl, my friend Steve's wife answered the phone, she was as shocked to hear my voice as I was relieved to hear hers. When I got to their home I told them of my fiasco in Hong Kong and that I was on my way back to New Hampshire. I was just about to ask if they could lend me some money so I could get back home, when they asked me to stay in Idaho.

Others had moved with them from New Hampshire and lived in their home and had been looking for work since they got there. I didn't want to burden these good people with my failure and problems, but they insisted, so it came to this. I said, "I will pick up that telephone book over there, and the first number in the yellow pages I see, I will call. If they hire me I will stay." I walked across the room and picked up the phone book and went to the yellow pages and put my finger down. Murphy & Sons cleaners is what I pointed my finger to. So I called, and was hired over the phone. I hung up

Stepping Out

the phone and said well, that, settled that. My friends were amazed, they had been beating the pavement for eight months trying to find jobs and I found one in the time it took me to walk across a room.

So I was cleaning supermarkets at night. I asked the owner of the company if I could use some of his window washing equipment during the day and I went door to door on my own, washing windows of store fronts throughout Boise. In two weeks time I had rented my own place, an apartment, and my wife and sons were arriving that next week. I think my wife was relieved she wasn't going to Hong Kong. Well, she and my sons joined me a week earlier than if everything had gone right in Hong Kong. We stayed in the apartment only one month when we found a farm house to rent, with barns and five acres of land, so we moved again. The farm house wasn't much but we worked the place and it gave back. We had chickens for fresh eggs and Nubian milking goats for milk and cheese. We also planted a large vegetable garden and bought a horse and saddle.

Idaho was a temperate climate paradise for me with mild winters in the valleys and hot dry summers. We spent the weekends in the mountains during the summer time. Weekdays I worked nights, I also gave up the window washing after a few months. Late afternoons my wife and oldest son and I would take turns riding our horse. Most of the time I got to ride two days a week.

Personally I was still suffering from my failure in Hong Kong. I knew I screwed up bad, God had showed me in a vision the person I had the dream about on the Japan Airlines flight before landing in Hong Kong; that I was to wait for and meet at the airport in Hong Kong was on the plane that I was told to get on in the first place in Canada. But God never allowed me to think or feel condemnation for my lack of faith. He just went right on working with me like a father teaching his child to walk. But I acted like a baby when he falls, when he is first learning how to walk. At this time the Lord was bringing understanding to me concerning the sacrifice of Abram in Genesis chapter 15, and the two edged sword of Revelation 1:16 and Hebrews 4:12. How the sacrifice of Abram was the sign of the voice of God; as his working of the two edge sword in my life is the sign of the inheritance of the land. It is also at this time while studying the seven messages of the seven churches of Asia in the book of Revelation that I saw in chapter 3:14 where it says.

>These things says to the Amen.

I saw by the spirit that Jesus had personified himself as the Amen as a noun. I knew Amen as an interjection at the end of a prayer. I was also aware of the Egyptian God Amen and always thought it peculiar, but never with much concern until now. I thought at first they have corrupted the Bible. I was at that moment in a state of panic. Then the LORD spoke to me and told me that:

> "Amen was the name Joseph knew me by and the
> name he told to Pharaoh, and that I was the GOD of
> his fathers, Abraham, Isaac and Jacob."

After hearing this I was greatly relieved and accepted what was spoken to me. But never the less knowing my GOD is the God of truth, he would expect me to try the spirits, so I did. The earliest recorded mention of Amen in Egyptian Mythology happens at the time around 1900 BC to 1567 BC. This is the proper time frame when Joseph would have been Vizier of Egypt. It is also within the time frame of the Hyksos. How many Pharaohs Joseph was Prime Minister for is uncertain, but those under his influence were known as the Hyksos Kings. This information is available at any good library.

The next things I looked at were the persona of the Egyptian God Amen. He was originally the invisible God and the creator God, father of all the Gods in Egyptian Mythology. This is identical to the persona and nature of the Hebrew patriarch's description of God, so I went on my way thankful to my GOD who continually takes pleasure in revealing his person to me and all those that love the truth.

Not coincidently within these great sustained dynasties of Egypt, from 1900– 1200 B.C., were the (Moses) Pharaohs. Ahmoses I 1570-1557 B.C., Tutmoses III 1475 B.C., Thutmoses IV 1401-1390 B.C. By which Moses of the Bible gets his name. Also

Stepping Out

there were the (Amen) Pharaohs at this same time as well.

It is entirely possible that these Pharaohs took their name titles according to their religious consciousness of either Amen or Moses as descriptive titles. A lot of study could go into this by Egyptologists. It would explain Amenhotep IV changing his name to Akhenaton and his monotheistic views as a result of events that took place in Egypt 200 years earlier. This caused his downfall and the enslavement of those with monotheistic consciousness that brought rise to the house of Ramses.

I was in Idaho about one year when I got news from the Lord that in New Hampshire a woman that fancied herself a prophetess was trying to convince a friend of mine to leave her husband because he wasn't a Christian (he didn't believe the way she did.) She had caused a lot of trouble in the past in these two people's marriage for some years. But now it was far more serious than her usual busy body antics. This time this woman was trying to convince my friend to leave her husband and take her share of the divorce settlement and give it to a pastor that was trying to start a Christian commune. My friend was very confused, whether to believe these people or honor her marriage, she really thought this woman was a prophetess and in her sincerity wanted to do the right thing. So I moved back to New Hampshire and confronted these people. There were a lot of hard feelings over all this and some friends were lost. But the last I knew my friend was still with her husband. Hopefully she has also learned to listen to God for herself instead of people claiming to be God's messengers, as I hope for everyone reading this book.

I stayed in New Hampshire for about a year and during that time I had several dreams of my own wife leaving me. I told the dreams to a friend that I worked with. I was worn down and asked God to give me a break it was all just too much. I felt I was carrying the whole world on my shoulders. I didn't want to accept these dreams I was having about my own wife. In these dreams she was determined to leave me and there was going to be nothing I could do. I was tired. I just wanted things to be good for us. I wanted to take care of myself and my family now.

I remembered how good it was in Idaho and wanted that kind of peace again. So I decided on my own to take a job on a dairy farm in New York State. The farm was right on Lake Champlain. So I began learning a new industry. I learned all I could and applied the knowledge from the dairy farm to my milk goats that I had purchased and was allowed to keep on the dairy farm. I just came to like goats milk better than cows milk. So I transferred the knowledge from the commercial dairy farm to my dairy goats to see what kind of improvement I could get from the goats. I stayed in this field of work for three years on three different farms. The last farm was in Virginia owned by the Land O Lakes Corporation.

I was a "herd manager" and was putting in ninety hours a week and my wife was putting in thirty a week on the same farm. We worked for a very nasty man that was hired by Land O Lakes to oversee the whole operation. The work load was just too much for me to handle. I decided to leave the farm so I took a job as a roofer's helper. This is how I came into my present trade and eventually a roofing contractor. That was sixteen years ago.

I started roofing for five dollars per hour in the Shenandoah Valley of Virginia. The work was brutal; we were removing existing roofs made of a product called coal tar pitch. When this stuff came in contact with skin or in your eyes, it usually caused first degree burns and sometimes second degree burns. The dust of this product would be like a cloud over the job site while we were removing it. Then, everyone would get burned from the foreman to the laborers, but the laborers burned far worse than anyone else on the roof. It was some kind of chemical reaction with the skin that caused this burning. After two weeks of this I decided I didn't want to be a laborer any longer than I had to be. I knew I had more brains than most of the people I worked with on the roof. So when we were sent out of town on a job, which was often, I would stay in my motel room and study technical manuals for whatever roof application we were doing at the time. The owner of the company was a good incentive for me. He was boasting he was going to be a millionaire in two years.

While I was studying, most of the guys I worked with were out drinking, buying the foremen beers, in the hopes he would assign them a good job the next day. My foreman was very competent and

Stepping Out

managed men better than anyone I have ever seen in the sixteen years I have been in the roofing industry. Within a couple of months I knew the specifications from the manuals better than my foreman. When I saw something not right developing on the roof, I would quietly bring it to my foreman's attention and suggest a remedy that would prevent future rework and make the job go smoother. This paid off much better than buying him drinks like everyone else was doing. I helped make him look good to the owner of the company.

When it was time to expand the company and start a new crew, I was made assistant foreman and within six months was running crews myself. My pay had doubled in less than eight months. Within a year I was free lancing myself and a crew to other roofing companies in Washington DC and Richmond Virginia. Those that came with me doubled their wages from the Shenandoah Valley. I was now making from sixteen to twenty-three dollars per hour. I was working fifty to sixty hours per week.

But at the same time it was taking a toll on my marriage and family life. I was always gone, I was out of town four or five days of the week. My two youngest sons would ask me to tell them of Jesus. I would always tell them not now, later. Later never seemed to come and their foundation years went by and I neglected to tell my two youngest sons of Jesus Christ.

This is my biggest regret in life. If there is anything I could have a second chance to do over in life this would be it. My sons are all men now and the two youngest are not Christians. They have Christian values, but that is not the same. They know I am Christian and their older brother is a Christian. But being family they see all our faults. They don't see much difference between us. This is my greatest mistake in my life to my shame.

I gained as much knowledge as I could in the roofing industry. I learned as many roofing systems as I could. I knew which system was the best system for any given project from California to Washington DC.

In May of '89 I returned to New Hampshire to start my own roofing company. I chose Conway, NH to set up shop. It was a fast expanding town in the Mt. Washington Valley, surrounded by National Forest. It has been my good fortune to have lived in many of the most beautiful places in the United States.

The first six months went well I was signing good project contracts. With good income, it looked like the house I had promised to build for my wife would be a reality within a year. Then the recession of 1990 came and everything dried up. No one was spending for roofs everyone was hunkering down waiting out the recession. I went to my wife and told her the situation we would have to delay starting the house until things picked up. I could get work at a roofing company in southern New Hampshire. When things got better, we could continue the plans for the house. She was having none of this she had just run out of patience with me. She told me I had robbed her of her youth, and then told me to leave.

I took the only option I had at the time, and took the job in southern New Hampshire. When I could find a roofing project of my own I would do it on weekends. My wife and I were still seeing each other but she didn't want to move to southern New Hampshire and she didn't want me in Conway except on the weekends. After two years of this I was feeling used. She was neglecting, or was unable to keep, the children in line. They began to start wilding and she couldn't keep them under control, yet she insisted on the status quo in our relationship. When I would go up to see them on the weekends if I wasn't working, she would just hand me a list of what they had done wrong and leave it to me to be the heavy. The children were beginning to resent me. All I was to them was the one who was the heavy that was going to drop the hammer on them. The whole scene was spiraling down further and further. One day while talking on the phone with her I was trying to convince her to move down south for the children's sake. They were wilding, their school grades had plummeted. They were staying away on weekends to avoid me. I hadn't seen any of my sons for nearly a month, but she would have none of it.

She said she liked the present arrangement and the children didn't want to live with me anymore anyhow, "This is the way it is so stop bitching about it just accept it." My two youngest sons were trying to convince their mother to divorce me because they knew this is what she wanted to hear. My oldest son did want us to work things out. I was examining my situation and the present status quo.

Stepping Out

The decision I came to was to file for divorce and head for a custody battle.

I hold no ill feelings toward my two youngest sons; if I had brought them up in the knowledge of the Lord, and had pointed them down the path to discover Jesus in their hearts as a good Christian father, all this would probably been avoided. My wife would not have been able to manipulate my two youngest sons, to play them like pawns, as so often happens in divorces. But we didn't get divorced yet, I had started no proceedings as of yet. I was still weighing the options, the pros and cons.

At this time I was working on a job in Walpole, Massachusetts and got into an argument with another roofer. One thing lead to another and he pushed me and I pushed him back and he landed on his ass. When he got up he picked up a tool, it was a tear bar used for removing old roofs, its like a five foot pry bar. He swung it at me and I raised my arm to deflect the blow. He swung again, and I went to lift my arm to block the blow again, but my arm wouldn't move. I took the blow squarely on the right side of my head, just above the right ear. The blow fractured my skull. Down to the roof deck I went. I don't know what happened next. I vaguely remember standing by the ladder but I don't know, I think I was going in and out of consciousness. I remember regaining consciousness and was unsure who I was, I just kept trying to remember. I remembered seeing my sons faces, but I struggled to remember their names. Once I did I just started reciting their names in hopes of preventing amnesia. The result of the blow to my head left me out of work for over a year. It took about four months to see again. I wasn't blind, but had double vision during this time. My motor skills were damaged and my speech as well. I stumbled to produce one word at a time, and the ringing in my head sounded like an electric generator running in my head. This lasted for three years. But the worst of all was the loss of the capacity to think in general. Everything was like peering into a fog, not knowing quite where you are.

I had to sue for workman's compensation. The company I worked for had fired me over the whole incident. They were claiming it was a personal argument. They hoped to avoid responsibility for the whole thing.

But I was the senior member of the roofing crew on the roof. The foreman had left with the implied understanding I was to keep things going in his absence.

My lawyer prevailed at the workman's compensation hearing, so now I had a settlement coming my way. The question now was, how much would that settlement be. This would be determined by the doctor's prognosis after a one year evaluation. My lawyer was talking about numbers in the hundreds of thousands of dollars for starters. The hearing to determine my eligibility came up about two weeks after the incident took place. My wife's attitude toward me changed as fast as my life just had. She invited me home to convalesce in Conway.

The next year went by fast, and my recovery was going reasonably well. The double vision had cleared up, my speech was returning, but slower than I would have liked. I sounded like a head injury victim. There was a head injury clinic close to Conway and a lot of the locals enjoyed making the people there the butt of their jokes. So I was really self conscious of my speech because of this. The ringing in my head was not diminishing. It was like being in a room with huge gasoline powered electric generators constantly running. Drinking alcohol was the only way to get relief from the turbines in my head.

I had made some new friends in town, mostly bartenders at first. One helped me get a job for the coming winter at the local ski area as a ski instructor. I thought the skiing and the interaction with people would further help my recovery, and hopefully at a faster pace. My final evaluation was coming up just before the start of the ski season.

Right around my birthday, the telephone rang; it was my lawyer with news. My doctor had submitted his final evaluation of his prognosis of my recovery to the insurance company. As my doctor had determined, my recovery was on schedule and he expected with all confidence, a full recovery on my behalf. My lawyer then explained that with this information and evaluation from my own doctor, my settlement was going to be drastically reduced. When he told me how much the insurance company was offering, he told me to take the settlement before they withdrew their offer all together. I took in a deep breath and sighed, and slowly hung up the phone, and went into the bathroom and took a shower. I just stood there with my head on the shower wall directly under the faucet, and I said to myself, "And now it begins." I showered, and got changed.

I then went into the living room and told my wife what my lawyer had just said. There is no other way to explain what my wife's reaction was to this news. It was amazing! I was instantly transformed, in her eyes, into an asshole again. This was the beginning of the end of my marriage. In the following weeks I could do nothing right in her eyes. I was taking a brow beating constantly for anything and everything. Then the accusations began; anything you can think of. I believe I am a patient man, but this was wearing very thin. There was no relenting on her part, and on one night of torture, while she was working to deprive me of sleep she threatened to cut off my testicles when I fell asleep. If she ever thought I was cheating on her, and she was talking as though that was what she was thinking. Well that woke me up in a hurry, and I left. Dwayne Bobbitt had just lost his and I was taking no more chances. I thought it might be something in the air at the time. I slept in my car that night in a supermarket parking lot. The next morning I went apartment hunting and found a place the same day. All I had was the clothes on my back. After a week or two my wife asked if we could try to work things out. I told her "Maybe, we'll see." With that she said good and told me I could take her to dinner the following Wednesday. I said "Maybe." She said "See you on Wednesday," and she left.

By now the ski season was half over and I had made new friends and was being introduced to new people everyday. Fresh faces with smiles and lots of good humor. It was really refreshing for me. Wednesday came around and some friends invited me to join them for dinner and drinks. I knew I had an implied date with my wife but my heart wasn't into it. So I joined my friends for dinner instead. When I arrived at my apartment later that night, after dinner, I entered and turned on the light. My wife was there. She had been standing in the dark waiting for me by the kitchen sink. "Where have you been?" she said. "We were to go out for dinner tonight." I told her I had already had dinner with friends. She gave me what had become the usual treatment with a few added obscenities. Then she stormed out of my apartment. I noticed she had something in her hand as she left. All that I had was one pot, one pan, one plate, one bowl, one spoon, one knife and one fork, and a couple of changes of clothes. So I followed quickly after her to the parking lot, outside of my apartment. I asked her what she had taken. "What's in your hand?" She raised her arm and brandished my carving knife and said "This!" I had had a few drinks at dinner and really wasn't taking her as seriously as I should have. I asked her snidely, "What do you think you are going to do with that." Her reply was "This!" She lunged forward and with a down stroke of her arm, with the knife in her hand. I reared back and pulled my left arm over my chest, to cover myself and I took the knife blow in my elbow, directly over my heart. I stepped back in shock. Then to my utter horror, she took the knife and cut both her wrists nearly to the bone in front of me. At that moment in time I knew she would die if I didn't get that knife from her hand. Even with all the things that happened in the past, both good and bad, I still loved her. I tried to get the knife from her, but she was swinging it wildly in front of her. I tried again. The knife came within millimeters of my face. I stepped back and took a deep breath and spun around and did a back kick. My foot landed squarely in her stomach and she flew through the air backwards for about ten feet and landed on her back. The knife went flying off into a nearby snow bank, and the wind was knocked out of her. I took my shirt off and tore it in half and tied off both her arms to stop the bleeding, then put her in her car and rushed her to the hospital. Luckily the hospital was only minutes away. When we arrived I carried her into the emergency room. When I came threw the doors even they were shocked. I was covered in blood from head to toe. I thought this was the darkest day of my life but things just kept getting worse!

At the hospital they were able to stabilize my wife, and when she was out of danger, they began to work on me. My stab wound was superficial in comparison to my wife. The nurse treated me like I was the scum of the earth, and I was half way feeling like that already. Really, I didn't need the attitude they were dishing out to me. I was beginning to get angry and I snapped back a rude remark

Stepping Out

to the nurses working on me. Just at that same time the police walked in. I told the police what happened, and the nurses listening rolled their eyes in disbelief. The police were just about to arrest me when my wife on the nearby operating table spoke up on my behalf and verified what I had told the police was the truth. The police finally took my statement and asked if I wished to press charges against my wife. I told them yes I did.

My wife was hospitalized for about a week. I was released that night. So it was left to me to tell the children what had happened. I told them the next morning. The first thing they asked me was, if their mother would live and I told them she would. I also told them I was pressing charges for attempted murder. My children pleaded with me not to put their mother in jail. After a long talk with them, we decided I would drop the charges if she wouldn't contest a restraining order and agree to counseling under a doctor's care. They agreed and in the end she agreed. So, I called the police to drop the charges against my wife. They asked me to come down to the station and when I arrived they were livid with rage towards me, and threatened me with perjury charges if I didn't follow through with the attempted murder charges. I got a little heady with them and told them in no uncertain terms I knew enough about the law that they could not make me testify against my wife. I told them I have read the Constitution of the United States of America and I know the Bill of Rights. They were very unhappy with me, but to their credit, they never harassed me for my decision so I thought.

My children came to live with me in my one bedroom, studio apartment. While their mother was recovering in the hospital, that first night was extremely difficult to deal with emotionally. I had to feed my children one at a time because I only had one pot, one pan, one plate, one bowl, one fork and one spoon. After feeding all of them my youngest son, twelve years old, at that time was sitting on the bed. I was leaning on the kitchen sink, then he asked me "Dad, are we poor?" It was just too much; I did all I could to not breakdown and cry. I turned around and faced the kitchen sink as if I was washing dishes while I was regaining my composure. Then I turned back to him and told him "No", we are just having a bad time right now. Everything will be all right. Things will get better, you will see." He believed me and they did.

Only a couple of days had passed since all that happened when I went to visit my wife in the hospital. I told her I had dropped the charges against her at the children's request, so long as she agreed to the restraining order and counseling. She refused. I told her "It's this way or it is jail. It's your choice." She got really angry, and told me I would have to take the kids permanently. I simply agreed. "Sure, no problem" I told her. When I left the hospital I thought to myself sarcastically, well that went real smooth! That day I went and rented a two bedroom condominium. It was fully furnished included kitchen supplies, dishes, pots and pans, etc.

When she was released from the hospital later that week she had the two youngest go back with her at her beckoning. My oldest son had gotten his own apartment. A week or two had gone by when I received a phone call from her. It was the night before our court hearing. She wanted to persuade me to drop the hearing for the restraining order and move back in with her. I told her I needed time away from her to let the dust settle, to let the waters calm, then, we will see.

But if the judge was to see things my way I would have him put the restraining order in place. I didn't want to find her waiting in the dark for me again. I told her we needed time to heal, and I needed to feel safe before I could live with her again. She told me she would love me forever and there was no need for a restraining order and said goodbye and hung up the phone.

The next day at court she asked me not to go through with the hearing. I refused; I truly felt I needed the restraining order for my own protection. She was still acting in the same way as before the incident, always dictating terms. I saw no difference and no remorse in any of her actions. I wanted the judge to force her to get help.

At the hearing the judge saw things my way and enforced the restraining order, and ordered my wife to undergo counseling under a doctor's care. He then went a near unprecedented step farther and divided our assets right there on the spot. She got both cars; all the household items, the furniture and child support from me and the bank account. I was allowed the part of my settlement money, about

Stepping Out

thirty five hundred dollars, and my tools for work. When we left the court, she told me in the parking lot, we were through and I would regret what I had just done. Then she drove away and I bundled my face from the cold and walked home.

After a couple of months, things seemed to have quieted down. I thought of calling her to see if she felt the same way. I decided to call the next morning. In my waking moments of that morning, the Lord came and spoke to me. He told me she had taken up with another man, and my marriage was over. I was heartbroken, and the Lord sent angels to uphold me and minister to my heart. I also realized it was the first time in nearly seven years since I had recognized the voice of the Lord, and I thanked him for that. Not since those days after returning from Idaho; when I asked him to let me alone, when I had said to him I needed a break, had I heard his voice. I think if he had not sent those angels, I would have gone out of my mind that day. I would have been a goner. He came to me that day to prepare my heart for what was to come. I called her that evening instead of that morning, and everything was as the Lord had said. She bragged about her new boyfriend until she was out of breath. Then I wished her happiness and hung up the phone and closed a chapter in my life in sorrow.

CHAPTER 14

Skating Again

I was grief stricken and couldn't even talk to other women in that way. I just wanted a friend, and I thank God that at this time in my life a woman named Susann was there for me. We had started working at the ski area at the same time. She hated being called Susann and preferred to be called Sue. She helped me through the rest of that ski season, and to this day is a sister to me. Nothing sexual ever happened between us, though the whole ski area thought differently, but nothing ever did. She was just the kind of friend that everyone in their moment of despair wished they had. When the ski season ended, she went back to Cape Cod and I climbed into a bottle of rum. I was so lonely I ached. I was drunk nearly every night for nearly three months.

My ex-wife and my sons had moved into her new boyfriend's place about a month earlier. My sons and my ex's new boyfriend weren't getting along. He was trying to lay down to law to them. They were having none of it. They had been used to having it their way for some time now, even for the year I was at home convalescing. My ex-wife had thwarted my disciplining of the boys on every issue.

Their mother made the choice and told them to go live with their father. She called me and told me the kids wouldn't listen to her or her boyfriend, so they would have to live with me. I agreed and she sent them to live with me. It was just as well, the summer school vacation had started. My sons were emotionally scarred by their mother's choice of her boyfriend over them. They had been loyal to her through all that we went through they now felt betrayed. I hurt for them. I understood their pain. But for me, I now see it as a God send: and God's way of saving me from alcoholism.

I hadn't done my trade, roofing, in nearly eighteen months since the day I had my skull fractured. I was just learning how to think again, never mind run a job site. I had been working at a lumberyard for about a month when my sons came to live with me. I was a yard dog. I stacked lumber, etc. and helped load building supplies for customers, but I was also meeting building contractors, restaurant owners and was getting a lot of leads on roofing jobs. Within a month I had signed enough work to last until the winter. All three of my sons worked for me that summer. They were learning a trade and just what it takes to make it all work. Some of the lessons they learned that summer may have seemed harsh to them at the time, but as they grew in understanding, they realized they were necessary. When school time came around my two youngest went back to school. My oldest worked with me until winter came and I shut the roofing down until spring again. I went back to ski instruction at Mt. Cranmore

The Lord was pricking my conscience little by little, more and more every day all through that summer. I was still drinking too much, but less and less week by week. God was bringing back dreams I had years ago with new understandings. I was testing these new understandings with the scriptures and they were passing the test. God was saying something to me.

Over the next four years my roofing company flourished. I was living a comfortable life again, but I was quite concerned with what the Lord was bringing back to me with these new understandings. I also kept receiving an awareness of the words of Jesus,

> "To whom much is given, much is expected: To whom little is given little is expected."

Also:

"He that has, more will be given to him and he that has not, even that what he has will be taken from him."

The Lord was bringing these sayings to me daily at nearly any part of the day, right out of the clear blue. My business increased and my drinking steadily decreased to nearly nothing. All during this time I was receiving more and more knowledge and understanding from the Lord. Always with the awareness,

"To whom much is given much is expected."

"Lord, what do you want me to do?" I asked, but got no reply. Life went on and again,

"To whom much is given much is expected."

Again I asked, "Lord what would you have me do?" But again, I received no answer.

I had tried several times to make a go of it with different women, all with good intentions at the start, but it always ended badly, but overall, life was good. I hadn't been with a woman for close to a year for one stretch. My friends enjoyed ribbing me about that, but truly, it was for lack of trying. I had searched my soul and after eighteen years of marriage I knew I wasn't wired to be a monk.

While working on a roof over a retail store one particular day, I saw a woman moving clothing from a retail clothing store into a warehouse nearby. She is really beautiful. I said to myself, "I've got to check this out." So I climbed down the ladder to get a better look. I was as dirty as a roofer can get, I mean I was grimy and she was dressed so fine. I walked by and made eye contact and said something stupid. I think it was "It's really hot today, isn't it." She only smiled, but I got to take a look at both her hands and she wasn't wearing a wedding band. I thought to myself, "That's good news," and walked around the corner of the building to a soda machine, and got sodas for every one on the roof. On my way back to the

The Way of Melchizedek

ladder, she was still there. So I struck up a conversation. She acted friendly by uninterested and I went back up the ladder to work. When she had finished what she was doing and was leaving, she looked up to the roof in my direction and smiled, while she drove away. I thought to myself, this calls for more investigation. I live in a small town and had never seen her before. I knew where she worked from our conversation, so a couple of days later I had to go to Portland, Maine to deliver some roofing tiles to an architect, so I dressed particularly well that day, and stopped by where she worked to say hi, and generally see where it would go. When she saw me she was really surprised and maybe a little impressed, that was my motive. She made mention how I was dressed. I said, "Yah, I know, I get really dirty on the job, but I clean up well." She laughed. I explained I was going to Portland to deliver samples to an architect, "it's the more pleasant side of my job." In our conversation I asked her if she was married. She said, "On paper maybe," with a laugh. I thought she was long separated or going through divorce. I asked her out for a drink, she declined politely and said she doesn't go out. We talked a little longer and I told her I had to get going, "See yah." She said bye.

In the next two weeks I bumped into her several different times yet I had never seen her before that day on the roof. The last of this series of times was in a department store. I told her "We have to stop meeting like this." She laughed. We talked a little. As I was preparing to leave I said "I would still like to take you out to dinner." She said that would be nice. I was pleasantly surprised, and we arranged a date for that coming Friday night. I took her to a place called the Stonehurst Manor. It was owned by a friend of mine. He was one of the first people to sign a roofing contract with me when I started roofing again after my head injury. The Manor was once the summer residence of the Bigalow family. In their hay day they were the largest importers of oriental rugs in the United States. It is a really nice place, with great ambiance and good food. I told the owner I was coming Friday night at 7:00 and I really liked this woman. He told me he would take care of everything. Friday came, dinner was great, the conversation was pleasant. But, at that time, I found out she was still living with her husband, and he was out of town for the weekend. I should have bailed out right then and there, but I listened to her story. No communication in over a year, separate bedrooms...I am not using this as an excuse. Truly, at that moment I said in my heart if King David can have Bathsheba and six hundred other wives also, and get away with it, why shouldn't I be able to have this woman. I don't have anyone. I thought to myself, "I really like this woman; she's smart, she's pretty; we get along great." So that was the start of that.

I should have read that section of the Bible again just to remind me what a terrible price King David paid for that decision.

I didn't just sleep with her. I took her from her husband. It crushed him. At least Uriah died with his honor and never knew or felt the pain and the shame I put this man through. All my life I will regret doing this to him and hope I never do such a thing ever again.

She's a good woman and was a dream to live with. She treated me with lovingness, dignity and respect. We were together for seven months and never had a cross word between us. We understood and respected each other's work and opinions, no matter how trivial the issue was. I have hurt her I am sure, and if things could be different, I would be very happy with her. But at the moment I rationalized and justified myself with what King David did. My life was turned upside down.

Jobs that I was bidding on I started to lose; over a couple of hundred dollars difference, even though the clients knew my work to be superior to my competitors. This was happening over and over even when I was low bid, I wasn't getting the jobs. Even jobs that were engineered and specked out for my benefit by the architects and project managers; jobs that everyone in town thought was a done deal for me, all fell though at the last moment. I was scrambling to find work, and the work I got was only enough to cover the bills. At the same time the stocks I had invested in took a nose dive, losing ninety percent of their value almost overnight.

After about three months I took a job I expected it to last six weeks. Ten weeks later we were almost done that last building, and I was complaining to my oldest son how little amount of money we made on this project. I optimistically said it can't get much worse than this. In less than a half an hour later I stepped on a steel roofing panel and it broke free from the roof. I fell down landing on the panel while it was sliding off the roof. I rode the panel off the roof. I hit the ground, and hard! My leg was broken, the job still unfinished, winter was coming and my life savings were wiped out.

I had no workmen's compensation on myself, only on my sons. "I'm finished," I thought. Interestingly enough, the building I fell off of was one of the Stonehurst Manor buildings where I tempted GOD with my King David rational, and decided to take another man's wife some five months earlier.

My sons pulled through for me and finished that job and the two other ones we had signed contracts for. I was at home with my leg elevated contemplating my situation and watching the stock I had invested in drop to nine cents per share. About a month had passed since I had broken my leg. I knew I had screwed up, sitting at dinner six months earlier at the Stonehurst Manor. Then the Lord spoke to me and said:

"To whom much is given, much is expected"

I asked the LORD, "What should I do! I am afraid the only thing left is my life." And he spoke and said again,

"To whom much is given much is expected."

I had heard this so many times...I said "What do you want me to do Lord!" Then I saw a vision of me writing a book of what the LORD had been showing me all of these years. And he said: "I will show you even greater things," and then he told me, "It is not permitted for you to have her."

I said, "But so many other people do this and nothing happens to them. Why me?" And he said "Because you are mine and I correct those I love, and I change the hearts of those who are mine." That night when JoAnn came home from work I couldn't face her to tell her. A week went by, it was Saturday. I had been struggling with what was before me to do. I loved her. I wasn't worried for her; she had a good job and was more than happy to take care of me if I couldn't find work.

Skating Again

But what of me, I had no where near enough money to stay in New Hampshire for the winter, and if it's a hard snowy winter, I would be looking for handouts from my family and friends, or freeze to death.

I had taken several vacations to Spain over the last three years. I had just enough money I could rent an apartment and winter there. The climate would be good for the healing of my leg and I could start writing the book I saw in my vision. I kept this thought in my head and that week went by.

The town I visited in Spain is called Almunecar, and it has an observatory. I would need an observatory at my disposal, to verify calculations in the book I was to write. I was considering all these things while I was surfing on the computer and looking up how my stock had done that week. It had rebounded to eleven cents. I shut the computer down in disgust. I was still out about one hundred thousand dollars.

Then I took my crutches and hobbled up the stairs to watch some TV, murmuring to myself on the way, "Tom what the hell are you going to do!" I turned on the television and the Breeder's Cup horse race was just getting underway. I thought, great, I like watching horse racing. This will be a good way for me to take my mind off of everything even if it is just for a moment.

The Breeder's cup is an end of the year race of all the best horses of that year's racing season. Well, the horses were walking to the starting gate. Then the announcer who was calling the race was giving the pre race run down on each horse, and their odds, and a little history of each horse in the race. As I am watching and listening to him as he gave the stats on each horse, there came this horse by the name of Spain. The announcer said it was a fifty to one long shot, the widest odds on a horse ever to be entered in the history of the Breeder's Cup. He went on to say this horse was not to be taken seriously and that the horse didn't even belong in this race, and that it was completely out of its league and out classed. At hearing this I said, "Lord, if you want me to go to Spain and start writing this book, have this horse named Spain win this race."

This horse was in a race against the cream of the crop, the winner of the Kentucky Derby the winner of the Belmont Stakes and the Preekness races, Horses of the highest caliber.

All the horses were loaded into the starting gate, the bell rang and they were off. I wasn't giving much thought to what I had just said. I just watched with near boredom. But coming into the last turn, Spain was very near the front or in the lead. Anyone who knows anything of horse racing knows in a long race, this is the worst place for your horse to be. I said to myself he's all done. But at the start of the home stretch, instead of losing ground, coming out of the back turn he had taken a clear lead. Now, what I had said a minute or two ago thundered back at me. My jaw nearly hit the floor. This horse was still accelerating and widening his lead. He crossed the finish line and won the race like he was the only horse in it. I sat there in silence, dumb-founded for a moment then said; "Okay, I will go to Spain".

That weekend I told JoAnn my decision that I was leaving for Spain on the first flight I could afford, and my youngest son was going with me. She took the news hard but never got angry, and our last three weeks together were better than the first.

I hope with all my heart and for the rest of my life that I am never again the catalyst in a struggling marriage that causes the ultimate end of any union between two people. God said there are six things he hates and the seventh is an abomination to him. That is, he that sew discord among families. I hope never again.

I left for Spain on January 12th of 2001 and stayed there for eighty-nine days. In that time I was able to lay out the initial format and about one hundred pages of first draft hand written copy and reference notes for other parts of the book. Far less than I hoped would be done by the time of my return to the United States. I had years of events and revelation to put in order. Luckily, many of the visions and dreams I had written down over the years.

The observatory in Almunecar wasn't much help to me. Their computer program was basic, and the language barrier also impeded my progress. All the calculations had to wait until I returned to the United States.

We returned to the USA on April 10, 2001. My youngest son and I stayed at my oldest son's house for a week. I already had three good sized jobs lined up; the contractors who had called wanted me

Skating Again

to get started on them right away.

I had to go see JoAnn and return her house keys to her, so I went to where she worked in town and when I saw her she cried with joy to see me again, and my heart melted like wax. Instead of returning her house keys to her, I was moving back in with her. In my heart I was hoping the Lord would allow or at least wink at what I had done for compassion's sake. But it wasn't to be. All the jobs that I had lined up fell through nearly instantly. I was advertising in every newspaper within a fifty mile radius, but the outcome was always the same. If I was low bid, the clients would decide to do the jobs themselves, or I just never heard back from them at all. I had never advertised so much in all my life but continually came up empty. The Lord wasn't letting me off the hook, and if it hadn't been for his past promises he had declared to me, I would probably be dead right now. His mercy is everlasting, and his mercy is even found in his justice.

Nearly three months had passed and I hadn't found any work with all the advertising I had done, the doors were all shut to me and that was the way it was.

I submitted myself to His will, and made arrangements to repair an old summer cottage my mother owned that had fallen into disrepair over the years. I had no money. Even if I had wanted to rent a place of my own, and I knew staying with JoAnn was only going to prolong both the drought of work and the inevitability of my submission to His will rather than my will. Nearly the moment I submitted; as I was driving my truck, an acquaintance flagged me down and asked me to help him roof a new house he was building. I told him I would and from that moment I set in my heart that JoAnn and I could only have a friendship on a platonic basis work started coming in. I had the cottage ready in about two weeks.

Within 24 hours of moving in I got two jobs and started on one immediately. Before I had finished it I had two more, and it looked like I would be busy through the rest of the summer, just like that. I thanked God for being patient with me and I worship him for all his long suffering towards me. For in all things what I am learning no one can resist his will and all things he set out to do will be done, and every knee shall bow and every tongue will confess that Jesus

Christ is Lord to the glory of the Father. As for myself, I am the Lord's and believe I am coming to the understanding of Jesus' statement,

> "who so ever shall fall on this stone shall be broken:
> but who ever it shall fall on it will grind him into powder."

This is for whatever purpose he so chooses. Whether to be blown away, like dust in the wind, or to be mixed with water to be fashioned into whatever kind of vessel that pleases him, whether a vessel of honor or dishonor.

He and He alone is righteous and all things that are made are made by Him and made for Him for what so ever purpose he chooses. For me, I acknowledge this; there is no wrong in Him. I look to his mercy towards me even as he said his mercy to me will be measured by my mercy to those that are brought into my life. What so ever he does with me makes no difference there is no fault in Him, may His will be done. As the summer was drawing to a close, a friend of mine and I were discussing astronomy. He had very advanced programs, far better than the computers in Almunecar, Spain, and even better than the Christa McAuliff Observatory in Concord, NH. I was finally able to test the revelation and visions I had concerning Orion, Sirius, and Leo and the psalm of David, psalm 19:1:

> The heavens declare the glory of God: and firmament tell of His handiwork."

The visions matched with the facts of astronomy down to the finest details. I was in total awe of God as detail after detail proved true, even as I have related them to you in the first half of this book.

The Lord has shown me the connection that Orion indeed was and is the astronomic representation of Jesus Christ and proved it with science even as He has allowed me to share this with you. The relationship with Jesus and those that believe in him is told every day in the night sky by God himself with his creation, and is proclaimed by his handiwork of Orion and Sirius and Leo. Even as the rising of Orion is three days, so was the Lamb of God in the heart of the earth three days. Also, the timing of the summer solstice and the flooding of the Nile, in concert with the gift of Pentecost and the Holy Spirit are in concert with the rising of Sirius. In all these things, all my visions were proven true. The connection of Leo rising 50 days after Passover and 47 days after Jesus' resurrection by using Orion's risings as the point of reference was perfect. This shows Leo as the glorified King of Kings. God united in man and all power in heaven is given to Him. All that I had hoped in these visions was confirmed even in greater detail than I expected.

For the next couple of weeks I was sorting the data from the astronomy programs and its star charts in concert with the visions I had received in the past so to present it in a somewhat orderly fashion to the public, in this book. Not such as easy task. There were so many avenues of thought all converging to a single hub, it was like the spokes on a wheel. Where to begin? They were all converging simultaneously and I am not quite sure if I have assembled all this converging information in an orderly fashion, but I have done what I could.

On August 22, around 11:00 in the morning, as I was putting on a new roof as is my trade, I looked upwards to the sky and saw in a vision, night instead of day, and I saw the constellation of Orion followed by the star Sirius which was followed by the constellation of Hydra with the constellation of Leo close behind Hydra, and the foot of Leo was poised to step on the head of Hydra.

In that moment, the Lord opened my eyes. In an instant, and simultaneously, I saw Orion as God in the Garden of Eden, and also as the Lamb of GOD at the same time, and I saw the star Sirius as the bride of the Lamb of GOD and at the same time as Adam and Eve and I saw the vision of the bride of God with the crown of the twelve stars of heaven clothed in the sun with the moon under her feet and as she brought forth the gift of union of the bridegroom and the bride. Then Hydra the Serpent came to devour the bride of God and her child. Then I saw Leo as the child of the union of the bride and the bridegroom at the same time He was the Lion of Judah resurrected in full power and Glory the Lord Jesus Christ, and he had victory over the serpent and death and he stepped on the serpent's head driving it into the ground and it bruised his heel but he crushed the serpent's head.

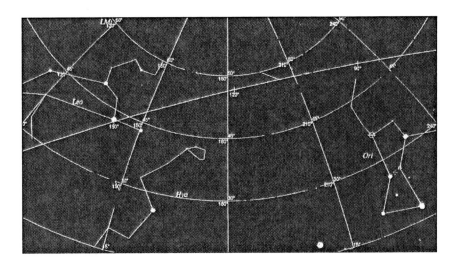

> The Lord God said to the serpent, because you have done this thing you are cursed above all cattle, and above every beast of the field; upon your belly shall you go, and **the dust of the earth** you shall **eat** all the days of your life. (man was made from the dust of the earth) I will put enmity between you and the woman, and between your seed and her seed; it shall bruise your head, and you shall bruise his heel. Gen 3:14 -15

Again, my being was filled with the knowledge: The heavens proclaim GOD'S glory and the firmament shows his handiwork.

I understood I had seen what John had seen and I worshipped the Most High, GOD creator of heaven and earth.

After this I marked August 22 as a holy day for me and I said I would not drink, alcohol and I would avoid women until I had accomplished my task of writing this book, and the next woman I have it will be with all my intent that she will be my wife for all the rest of the days of my life. So, the monk I am not wired to be, I was. Until the Lord accomplishes in me the task he has set before me.

When I read this night sky from right to left as the Semitic languages are written on paper, I realized this vision I had this day was the complete history of mankind put in the sky like a cosmic movie screen that begins with Eden traveling through time and finishes with the Kingdom of God on earth. This is the testimony and promise of the Most High arced across the sky from the beginning of time. This is the Ark of his Testament found in Revelation 11:19 and then described and explained in Revelation chapter twelve and onward it is there for all that are willing to know the way. This is the message that has been televised from the creation of the universe and told by the priesthood after the order of the way of Melchizedek.

> The heavens declare the glory of GOD: and the firmament shows his handiwork day after day it utters speech night after night it shows his knowledge. There is no speech nor language where their voice is not heard.
> Their good news has gone out throughout all the earth and their words to the end of the world. He has set his tabernacle in the sun among them. And he is a bridegroom coming out of his chamber and rejoices as a strong man to run a race. Psalm 19: 1-5.

So, I thank God for what he has brought to me and I share it with you, as He has commanded me to do. He that turns to God and makes the teachings of Jesus Christ the compass of their hearts and look only to Him in this time of trouble that is now coming to the earth are those that follow his ways, they will not be ashamed in the hour of judgment.

On the morning of the first day of the week, on September 9, in the year 2001, around 7:00 I was meditating on the words that the Lord had put into my understanding and again he filled my understanding and that is; those who's eyes of their understanding that

He has opened, shall see him the Lord in all their fellow humans. The moment of truth of this understanding of one's faith is when your life is on the line; will you kill another to save your own skin (your shell), that is to say, your own body, in hopes of saving your own life? At that moment he spoke to me in a vision, in many visions all at the same time, and said;

> "If you kill them that come to kill you for My sake, whom you profess to see as containing My being, then you are even as they that come to take your life? In so doing you make your witness of me a witness of unbelief. Can the yoke of an egg strike out at the shell of another? You, knowing my good gifts, asked of Me for an egg and I have given this to you. I have not given you a scorpion".

As this was spoken I knew this was the acid test. Here is where my faith in the resurrection and my witness of Jesus Christ is tested. This is where the rubber meets the road. I then saw God in a vision blessing Noah as he left the ark after the great flood. Then He said to Noah,

> "Whoever sheds the blood of men by man shall his blood be shed: for man was made in the image of God."

At the same time I saw Jesus giving his Revelation to John saying,

> "If any man has an ear let him hear. He that leads into captivity shall go into captivity. He who kills with the sword must be killed with the sword." Here is the patience and the <u>faith</u> of the saints.

Even at the same moment as all these visions filled my being I saw and heard him say,

"I counsel thee to buy of me gold tried in the fire that you may become rich: and white raiment that the shame of your nakedness is covered. Anoint your eyes with eyesalve that you may see on the day of my visitation. As many as I love I correct and chastise be zealous therefore and repent. Behold I stand at the door and knock if any hear my voice and open the door. I will come in to him and sup with him and he with me. To him that overcomes will I grant to sit with me on my throne, even as I have overcome and sit with my Father on his throne."

All this came to me that morning and all at the same moment in time even as my consciousness received all these visions from all directions all simultaneously.

As I was acknowledging his truth and wrestled with the unbelief in my own flesh, I prayed if this moment of truth came upon me, that my life is to be tested at the hands of my persecutors His Spirit prevails in me, and that I also may overcome for my life rests in Him.

As I thought on all these things while I looked out my window toward the eastern sky, I saw in a vision the very fabric of the sky as a curtain being sliced open and the sky gave way in an instant and the Lord Jesus came in power: and all the realm of heaven with Him and He thrust through the curtain of the sky and He filled all the space of this world in less than a second and his people were delivered and their persecutors were vanquished and the governments of earth were overthrown and the earth was soaked in the blood of his enemies. Then I saw in a vision, a new born baby being circumcised, and the head of the child's penis popped forth, instantly after the circumcision was completed and it was bloody; covered in blood. The Lord spoke, and my being was filled with his word,

So shall it be for all flesh of the earth, on the day I circumcise the earth.

I do believe this day is coming and soon and I pray I will be watching for him. My observation is this: it is the lack of faith in the promise of God that causes man to build their great religious institutions with their grandiose cathedrals, and their synagogues and mosques within their clerical hierarchies as the place to worship God. They neither know nor understand the statement: "Can anything good come out of Nazareth"? You are the town of Nazareth! You within your own self that is that place known for good-for- nothingness and from out of this is where the Messiah is to come. This is the promise. They the fearful and unbelieving despise this notion, and in their own hearts can not comprehend it to be so but yet it is. They also do not understand why God changed Abram's name to Abraham, or Jacob's name to Israel. But the meaning of this is revealed in the syllables of their names, and thunders with the statement "Can anything good come out of Nazareth..." Come and see.

The way of Melchizedek is not another denomination to be joined; with an administrated organization under the control of men in this world, to do so would be blasphemy of his prophesied promise. It has no buildings to worship within after the manner of temples and synagogues, cathedrals or mosques; made with the hands of humans and never will have. It is a different way it is those that worship the Most High God in the sanctified place of their own heart. They are those who have the gift of faith; forming Christ in them by his living word engrafted in them transforming their inward parts. These have the spark of life by union with his Spirit in them. They are the union. Religion has butchered the message he has declared in his gospels; they have scattered his body in pieces through out the earth. My wish for all is that you read his gospels Mathew, Mark Luke and John in particular for yourselves if you can believe in your heart he is the Living God and **his teaching** finds a place in your heart he will be your Lord and Savior.

The second coming of the Lord Jesus is truly at hand. The time of the Gentiles is nearly fulfilled. I wait with expectation for the day of our deliverance and the promises the Lord has made to me to be fulfilled in the glory of His kingdom. Yet for me it is his next moment of his coming in my heart I look to; his light shining out of my own darkness and the opening of my eyes to his understanding. By this are the steps of my feet guided, as my preparation to His glory continues in me. May his light also shine in you. AMEN

Though I have all knowledge to understand all mysteries in heaven and on earth whether by visions or dreams but do not express the mercy provided by his Christ by which we all will judge ourselves I am nothing more than a hollow chime. Follow his mercy one to another and you will be perfect before God, in this world and the world to come. This is true knowledge and true wisdom. Who so ever dreams a dream or has a vision or revelation that does not lead to his expression of love it is false; false knowledge and false wisdom it is idolatry. God will remove this from his presences. Love one another forgive one another.
1st Corinthians 13

Printed in the United States
17622LVS00002B/232-237